Twayne's English Authors Series

Sylvia E. Bowman, *Editor*

INDIANA UNIVERSITY

Christopher Smart

(TEAS) 161

CHRISTOPHER SMART

By FRANCES E. ANDERSON

Creighton University

Twayne Publishers, Inc.   ::   New York

Library of Congress Cataloging in Publication Data

Anderson, Frances E.
  Christopher Smart.

  (Twayne's English authors series, TEAS 161)
  Bibliography: p.
  1. Smart, Christopher, 1722-1771.
PR3687.S7Z57   1974   821'.6   73-15943

ISBN 0-8057-1502-9

PR
3687
.S7
Z57
1974

Preface

Christopher Smart, an eighteenth-century poet who wrote some of the finest religious and lyrical verse in English, has been relatively little known; and his small fame has been based, for the most part, on his masterpiece, *A Song to David*. During the twentieth century, however, scholars and critics have shown increased interest in Smart. New appraisals and appreciations have been written concerning not only the *Song* but also his other work. An important addition to his canon, *Jubilate Agno,* was discovered and published; recent biographies and editions have also helped to establish his literary reputation.

The poet's early work and career were along conventional lines, and Smart was accepted with some appreciation by his contemporaries. His later and best work, written after his release from confinement in a madhouse, seemed unconventional and was rejected by most of Smart's critics and friends. In addition, his strange religious activity and fervor—the motivating force in his poetry—alienated him from many of his literary companions and friends; this alienation continued, with a few notable exceptions, until the poet's death.

Yet Smart's writings and other activities—strange as they may have seemed to his contemporaries—had much of the deliberation, order, and precision, as well as many of the ideals, of the period. His steadfast attitudes of affection for his friends, of sympathy for the suffering, of regard for learning, of eagerness to help—in a pragmatic way—those in need, of seriousness concerning his work, and of devotion to his God—all are in the eighteenth-century tradition. Smart has been linked with Blake, and he shares much of the latter poet's idealism, imagination, and intellectual integrity. But Smart's poetic genius seems nearer that of Cowper, who also showed signs of madness, and who also overrode the artificiality of his period while retaining some neo-Classic features in his writing.

Cowper's and Smart's works are both characterized by the deep sympathy with nature, love of animal life, and concern for humanity found in Blake; but they have a more orthodox religious orientation. Smart is certainly, with Cowper and Blake, a forerunner of the Romantics; but his roots are in the eighteenth century—even though it rejected him. The attitudes of his contemporaries influenced greatly not only the poet's life and work, but also his literary reputation during his lifetime and for some time to come. Thus it seems appropriate to examine, in the first part of this volume, the political, social, and literary background of the century in which Christopher Smart lived.

The life of a poet and his poetry are always bound together, but in the case of Christopher Smart this statement is exceptionally true. As shown in Chapters 3 to 6, his experience, ideas, and attitudes from his earliest days are reflected in his poetry. After his struggling years with hackwork in Grub Street, and after his period of confinement, Smart became infused with one purpose; to exalt the goodness and greatness of God through his poetry. The second part of this volume is concerned with the poet's life and the factors affecting his career as a poet.

The last and largest section of this volume contains a critical evaluation of Christopher Smart's poetry, arranged chronologically, with special emphasis on the *Song*. Little comment has been included on his prose published in periodicals—much of it hackwork—and elsewhere, with the exception of some remarks on the critical preface to his verse translation of Horace. Only a few very general comments concerning his prose and verse translations themselves occur. There is still work to be done in finding and identifying Smart's work because the poet wrote under a number of pseudonyms.

Although Smart was an original thinker, he also drew from his extensive scholarship; and many of his sources have been indicated. But here again, even though some painstaking and valuable research has been accomplished, much remains to be done. Smart was a scholar and a wide reader; there are many of his references which still baffle readers and which make his work—based to some extent on "free association" —seem obscure. A short history of the progress of Smart's literary reputation from his own time to the present concludes this section.

Included in the bibliography are references to major editions of his work; to the eighteenth century—one of the great intellectual and fruitful periods in English literature; to some of the recent critical biographies telling the moving story of Smart, the man and his work;

and to some of both past and present criticism, including the citation of some recent articles showing the increased interest in works other than the *Song*.

All quotations from Smart's poetry—with the exception of lines from *Jubilate Agno,* edited by W. H. Bond, London, 1954, and published by permission of Rupert Hart-David—are taken from the *Collected Poems of Christopher Smart,* two volumes, edited by Norman Callan, London, 1949, and published by permission of Routledge and Kegal Paul, Limited. The University of Missouri Press has also granted permission for a number of citations from *Christopher Smart: A Biographical and Critical Study,* by Edward G. Ainsworth and Charles E. Noyes (*The University of Missouri Studies,* Volume XVIII, No. 4), Columbia, 1943.

FRANCES E. ANDERSON

The Creighton University
Omaha, Nebraska

Contents

Preface

Chronology

1. The England of Christopher Smart   15
2. The Life of Christopher Smart   22
3. Smart's Early Work   54
4. *Jubilate Agno*   70
5. *A Song to David*   78
6. The Last Works of Christopher Smart   103
7. Christopher Smart and the Critics   112
    Notes and References   125
    Selected Bibliography   130
    Index   137

Chronology

1722   Christopher Smart born in Kent.
1727   George II ascended the throne of England.
1733   Peter Smart, father of Christopher, died; the family moved to Ruby Castle in Durham.
1739   Smart entered Pembroke College, Cambridge.
1742   Smart won the Craven scholarship with a Latin translation of Pope's *Ode for Music on Saint Cecilia's Day.*
1744   Smart received his bachelor's degree.
1745   Smart was appointed Fellow of Pembroke Hall on July 5, 1745; three months later he was designated Praelector of Philosophy and chosen Keeper of the Common Chest.
1746   Smart was appointed Praelector of Rhetoric; he also served as tutor. Smart reprinted his translation of *Ode for Music on Saint Cecilia's Day,* accompanying it with his own *Ode to Music.* His *Ode to Music* was set to music by William Russell. In this year and the next, several short pieces by Smart appeared in Robert Dodsley's *The Museum.*
1747   Smart was granted a master's degree.
1748   Smart's *Ode to the King,* a Pindaric ode on the return of George II of England, following the War of the Austrian Succession, was published with other similar tributes in *Gratulatio Academiae Cantabridiensis.* A musical setting for his ode, *Idleness,* appeared.
1749   Smart left Cambridge for London.
1750   Smart began to publish material in *The Student;* he may have served as editor. He also won the Seatonian prize for his poem *On the Eternity of the Supreme Being.* In June, Newbery published Smart's *Horatian Canons of Friendship* under the

name of Ebenezer Pentweazle—the first of Smart's many pseudonyms. In October appeared a new monthly, *The Midwife* or *The Old Woman's Magazine,* a collaboration of Smart and Newbery.

1751   Smart became involved in a literary battle with William Kenrick, who attacked Smart in a satiric *Old Woman's Dunciad.* In March, Smart wrote an epilogue and prologue for an amateur performance of *Othello.* The poet again won the Seatonian prize with his essay, *On the Immensity of the Supreme Being.* In the autumn he began to work on a comic entertainment, *The Old Woman's Oratory,* which continued through 1752.

1752   Smart published *Poems on Several Occasions.* This year is the conjectured one of the poet's secret marriage to Anna-Maria Carnan.

1753   Smart brought out his *Hilliad,* a satiric Dunciad-like piece denouncing John Hill, who attacked Smart's poems. Smart's first child, Marianne, was born in May. In November, the dividend from Pembroke was withheld on news of Smart's clandestine marriage; but his name was kept on the college books so that he could compete for the Seatonian prize.

1754   Smart's second child, Elizabeth, was born. Some of his poems appeared in the *Gentleman's Magazine.*

1755   Smart won the Seatonian prize for *On the Goodness of the Supreme Being* and continued contributions to the *Gentleman's Magazine.* Plans were started to launch *The Universal Visitor.*

1756   Smart published *The Works of Horace, Translated Literally into English Prose* and *Hymn to the Supreme Being, on Recovery from a dangerous Fit of Illness.* The first issue of *The Universal Visitor* appeared in February. Although during this year Smart became ill and was later confined, his friends—among them, Samuel Johnson—continued to contribute to *The Universal Visitor* in Smart's behalf.

1757   *The Nonpareil,* a collection. of pieces from *The Midwife,* was published by Thomas Carnan, Mrs. Smart's brother and a member of Newbery's firm, probably for Smart's benefit. In May, Smart was sent to St. Luke's Hospital.

1758   Smart was discharged from St. Luke's in May, "uncured"; his wife and children left for Ireland where they established residence.

1759   David Garrick presented a benefit for Smart. The poet was again confined; it seems probable that *Jubilate Agno,* his madhouse manuscript, was started toward the end of the year. He possibly worked on other writings in addition to the *Jubilate.*

1760   George III ascended the throne.

1763   January is the conjectured date of Smart's release from the asylum. *Mrs. Midnight's Orations* was published. *A Song to David* was issued in April. Other publications were *Poems,* a pamphlet containing *Reason and Imagination, A Fable;* and *Poems on Several Occasions,* including *Munificence and Modesty.*

1764   The oratorio *Hannah* and the *Ode to the Earl of Northumberland, on his being appointed Lord Lieutenant of Ireland. . .With some other pieces* were published.

1765   Smart published *A Poetical Translation of the Fables of Phaedrus, with The Appendix of Gudius.* His long-awaited work, *A Translation of the Psalms of David, attempted in the Spirit of Christianity and adapted to the Divine Service* finally appeared. Friends of the poet compiled and brought out *A Collection of Melodies for the Psalms of David According to the Version of Christopher Smart, A.M. By the Most Eminent Composers of Church Music.* In November, Dryden Leach, the printer of his *Translation of the Psalms,* had him arrested for a debt of eighty-six pounds. Smart was rescued through the efforts of a "Friend."

1766   *The Domestic Entry Book* for April 26 contains a note that King George III intended to give Smart the next place of Poor Chevalier which should become vacant in the Chapel of St. George. The vacancy did not occur, but a pension of fifty pounds a year was procured for Smart.

1767   *The Works of Horace, Translated into Verse. With a Prose Interpretation, for the help of students* was published. In December, John Newbery died, leaving one-third of his estate to be held in trust for Anna-Maria Smart; one of the provisions required that "the same or any part thereof shall not be subject to the debt, power or control of her present husband."

1768   *Abimelech,* an oratorio, was published by Smart; he also brought out *The Parables of Our Lord and Saviour Jesus Christ.*

1769   Smart contested the will of Francis Smart on the grounds that he was heir-at-law, but in July he was obliged to sign an indenture showing that his position gave him no claim on Francis's estate.

1770   In April, Smart was arrested and taken to the King's Bench Prison, on charge of debt. In December, while he was still in prison, his *Hymns for the Amusement of Children* was published.

1771   Smart died in May in prison after a short illness. He was buried in St. Paul's Churchyard.

CHAPTER 1

The England of Christopher Smart

I *The Expansion of the Empire*

With the death of William III in 1702, Queen Anne ascended the throne of England and reigned until 1714. Her reign at the start of the eighteenth century marked the beginning of England's great effort to achieve political and economic supremacy throughout Europe and the world. During the early part of her reign, Marlborough, by his victories over the armies of Louis XIV at Blenheim (1704) and Ramillies (1706), saved England from domination by France. England had already established her supremacy on the sea by the naval victory at La Hogue (1692); later, she gained control of the western Mediterranean by the capture of Gibraltar and the island of Minorca. Other important victories strengthened England's supremacy: Clive's victory at Plassey (1757) resulted in British rule in India; Wolfe's capture of Quebec ended the power of France in Canada; and the capture of Fort Duquesne, afterward named Pittsburgh, determined that the territory west of the Alleghenies was to be developed by English-speaking settlers. This last victory, however, was offset by the American Revolution and by the British loss of her thirteen colonies in North America.

England's military success and political expansion had important results. London, a city of eight hundred thousand during the century, became the world's greatest seaport and financial center. The city also became the gathering place of most of the great literary figures of the day, and their subjects concerned many of the happenings which were shaping the life of the country. There developed a great middle class of merchants and tradesmen. Transportation of goods was made possible by the construction of a network of canals and by the paving of roads—especially roads to London.

II   *Science*

An important scientific publication of Queen Anne's reign was *Optics* (1704), by Sir Isaac Newton, the discoverer of the law of gravitation in 1686. From 1703 until his death in 1727, he was president of the Royal Society; and he was recognized throughout the Continent as Europe's foremost scientist. Other distinguished thinkers of the century included the Scottish philosopher, David Hume (1711-76) and Adam Smith, another Scotsman, who inaugurated the modern science of economics by his *Wealth of Nations* (1776).

These scientific discoveries and other events provided the main-springs for many of the changes of thought of the period. After the foundation of the Royal Society in 1660, the scientific experimenta-tion produced in the people's minds a belief in a universe of ordered and invariable law in which witchcraft and magic had no part. The idea of order permeated to the everyday living of the people; and reason, good sense, and good taste became the criteria. While there continued to be interest in religious questions, the obscure theology and metaphysics of the seventeenth century became of less concern.

III   *Social and Political Attitudes*

Another dominant idea of the century was humanitarianism, the interest in helping the unfortunate which ultimately led to prison reform, to the building of hospitals and asylums, and to the abolishment of slavery. Ideas of democracy, which began to make themselves felt, resulted in the American Revolution and the French crusades for liberty, fraternity, and equality. The same political unrest that later erupted into revolution on the Continent and in America occurred in England during the early part of the eighteenth century. The Whig and Tory parties carried on a continual struggle for power, and literary men of the period pressed the arguments of the two parties in a barrage of pamphlets and poetry.

The increase in the size of the reading public made this political material valuable, and the writing of such work became a means of securing advancement. Since the religious and political aspects of the parties were closely allied—the Tories were apt to be owners of large landed estates and supporters of the Established Church; the Whigs, merchants and Presbyterians of Scotland or members of the dissenting

Churches of England—the benefits of party patronage related to government and church. Thus a loyal clergyman might be made a bishop or dean, an influential pamphleteer rewarded by a good government position.

IV   *The Literary Scene*

Two prominent literary men of the period—Jonathan Swift and Joseph Addison—directed much of their literary efforts in support of their particular parties. Addison worked for the Whig cause; Swift, although he had been brought up a Whig, tried through his energies to help the Tory cause because he felt the Established Church in danger. But with the death of Anne and the Hanoverian succession—to which the Whigs gave allegiance—the country entered a period of comparative peace, with the Whigs in the ascendancy. Thus, during the reigns of George I (1714-27) and George II (1727-60), the efforts of the literary men were not so needed; and the court was a negligible part of the literary scene.

The attention of the writers of the eighteenth century was directed, therefore, to the everyday life of the individual and to the government of men and their concerns by right reason. This insistence on sober reflection and examination of values sought to prove a median between the extremes of Puritan prohibitions and Restoration license. The literary works of the day reflected the interests and happenings of everyday London as well as those of the English countryside with its villages and farms. Because the writers were seriously interested in forwarding their ideas of the need of reason and control in man's behavior, they tended to moralize. But the moralizing was not concerned with the other world but with the practical rules of living in this world.

The real and actual facets of life, then, became the material from which the writers of the eighteenth century wove the fabric of their work; as a result, flights of fancy and imagination held little value, besides being suspect. Occasionally a writer such as Swift depicted an imaginary island, Lilliput; but even this piece of fancy was closely allied to the situation of man in the universe as Swift saw it. Every effort was made to make such an imaginary part of the world seem as real as possible; the island in Daniel Defoe's *Robinson Crusoe* was supposed to be an actual place. And the efforts of Gulliver and Robinson Crusoe alike are directed toward the practical needs of food, shelter, and the like.

This faithful examination of the actual detail of the life of men of the day also produced some of the great biography of the period, notably James Boswell's picture of Samuel Johnson and his fellow writers and friends. The detailed relatings of happenings and the resultant thoughts became a part of the letters of the day; these writings give a valuable insight into the mind and life of the period. The personal letters of literary figures such as Thomas Gray and William Cowper, and the personal essays of Addison and Oliver Goldsmith became an introductory note and preparation for the most significant literary form of the period: the novel.

The novel became a form with great appeal for the rapidly widening circle of English readers, concerned as it was with human nature and social behavior—and not demanding anything more profound than ordinary understanding of persons and events. It often had as its hero a common man—a sailor, a country parson, or a doctor—a hero in accord with the growing sentiments of democracy. *Pamela,* by Samuel Richardson, called "the first English novel," is concerned with a servant girl and her struggle to defeat a scheming member of the higher classes. Because the plot is carried forward by letters, the action of Pamela is of less interest than the characterization. Henry Fielding's *Tom Jones* (1749) carried Tom through the English countryside, by wayside inns, to London. *Tristam Shandy* (1760-67), a novel by Laurence Sterne, has a group of humorous characters through whom the writer reveals his own personality and social attitudes.

The drama of the eighteenth century did not reveal the life of the times as significantly as did the novel, but there were contributions of note almost every evening at some of the well-known theaters of the day: the Covent Garden Theatre, the Drury Lane Theatre, and the Haymarket; lesser-known theaters provided some drama as well. One of the forms of drama most popular was the "sentimental comedy," as exemplified by Sir Richard Steele's *The Conscious Lovers* (1722). Reaction to the "sentimental comedy" vogue can be seen in Goldsmith's *She Stoops to Conquer* (1773), and in Richard Sheridan's two plays, *The Rivals* (1775), and *The School for Scandal* (1777)—all three plays successful on the stage. A still popular favorite is John Gay's *The Beggar's Opera* (1728).

Tragedy was not in keeping with the intellectual climate of the day;

there were some pretentious blank-verse tragedies, but they were not successful. Revivals of drama by Shakespeare, Ben Johnson, Francis Beaumont and John Fletcher were a little more popular, revised as they were to appeal to the prevailing taste. A prose drama, George Lillie's *The London Merchant* (1731)—a domestic tragedy of middle-class life—offered more interest to the rising middle class.

Not the tragic, but the comic—often satiric—spirit dominated the literature of the age. Humor and robust jest, the kindly wit of Addison, the brilliant satire of Swift in *Gulliver's Travels,* had as their subjects the foolish actions of men not governed by reason. Satires in verse, modeled on classic examples, were popular; Alexander Pope's "Epistle to Dr. Arbuthnot" and Johnson's "Vanity of Human Wishes" demonstrate the English adaptation of the formal satire.

The temper of the age, with its emphasis on the practical, the sensible, and the everyday, influenced the poets of the period. Most of the poetry of Pope, Gay, Cowper, and much of Robert Burns is concerned with this customary and conventional level of life. Bursts of enthusiasm met with disapproval. Smart felt the impact of this attitude when he published his *Song to David* and other religious poems after his confinement. Even when the typical writer of the period left the mundane for higher levels of thought, he usually used a stilted, grandiose diction which marred the poetic effect. This pseudo-elevated diction—sometimes found in the work of Gray, William Collins, and many of the minor poets—attempted to imitate the manner of John Milton. Other aspects of Milton's verse imitated by the eighteenth-century poets included inversion of normal word order and the use of personified abstractions such as "pale Envy."

From these pretentious mannerisms Pope, one of the most influential literary figures of the first half of the century, was, for the most part, free. His heroic couplet, used in his longer poems, was a favorite verse form of the day. Pope was also important in his defining of critical principles in his *Essay on Criticism.* Pope's criteria, labeled by literary historians "neo-Classicism," advocated the qualities of good sense, fidelity to the known facts, reasonableness, and keeping to the normal ideas of human nature; and the models of the neo-Classic writers were the Classical writers of antiquity who best seemed to hold to the principles of reason and truth in nature. Followers of these criteria scorned anything abnormal and outside human experience, especially adventures of an extravagant nature such as are shown in medieval romance. While the influence of Pope's neo-Classic ideals was beneficial in that it contributed to simplicity, clarity, and naturalness in writing, it was too narrow and restrictive. Human imagination must be free to roam beyond everyday experience and established, ascertainable fact.

Because Samuel Johnson, the leading literary figure of the last half of the century, also favored the neo-Classic theories, they continued to dominate beyond the middle of the century. Yet there were rebellious elements beginning to make themselves felt. The ideal of the superior civilized man—the product of reason, culture, and regulation—was opposed by a "noble savage" figure, who was free from the corruption of the cities in particular and of civilization in general. An essay by a French writer, Jean Jacques Rousseau, written in midcentury, suggested to eighteenth-century readers that scientific and literary progress had gradually had a corrupting influence on morals.

The English countryside, rather than Johnson's beloved London, became the center from which poets perceived truth untainted by the selfishness and materialism of town. The man of the soil and the villager became, with the "noble savage," idealized figures exemplifying the unspoiled children of nature. Inspiration, the spontaneous expression of feeling one might expect from the untouched peasant, became more essentially valuable than the products of reason.

Thus Thomas Gray's "Elegy Written in a Country Churchyard" had neo-Classic form and holds to neo-Classic principles of poetry, but its sentiments are in accord with this new sympathy and admiration for the countryman of lowly birth. Among the "rude forefathers" in the country churchyard there might be lying a Milton, who—because of poverty—had been unable to make his genius felt. Death, the great leveler, made equal those proud of high birth and accomplishment with the humble plowman and his busy wife.

The loss sustained when the rustic left his native village for the town is depicted in Goldsmith's "The Deserted Village." Cowper, essentially neo-Classic in style and tone, declared, "God made the country, and man made the town." Robert Burns, although influenced by the traditions of the Scottish poetry, took as his subjects the small animals of the field, the rural scene, and those men who roamed the hills. He used a rustic dialect—the language of the common man—and his satire and his commentary on man are different from the polished and sophisticated verse of Pope.[1]

V   *Christopher Smart and His Century*

At the beginning of his career, Christopher Smart (1722-71) and his work were both in accord with the orderly, disciplined, reasonable life of the major part of the eighteenth century. After his release from the madhouse, he was rejected both as a man and a poet. His irregular life, enthusiasm, sensitivity, highly emotional outpouring of feeling, and the unconventional quality of his verse jarred the sensibilities of his contemporaries. Smart was one of the precursors of the Romantic movement in his rebellion from determination by reason, rules, and objectivity of observed facts; he sought, as did William Blake later, a new expression for exalting the spirit of love. Yet Smart, like William Cowper, held to some of the neo-Classic ideals and conventional religious attitudes; he was an integral part of the eighteenth century.

CHAPTER 2

The Life of Christopher Smart

I Family

Christopher Smart was proud of his ancestry. He once described himself—in the preface to his verse translation of Horace—as "a gentleman derived from ancestors, who have abode upon their own Lordship, six hundred years in the County Palatine of Durham."[1] Traditionally, he was descended from Sir John Smart, Garter King of Arms under Edward the Fourth. Another of Christopher Smart's forebears was a Puritan zealot during the reign of Charles I, Dr. Peter Smart, whose protest against the renovation of Durham Cathedral caused him to be deprived of his preferments and to be fined and imprisoned for ten years in the King's Bench Prison. More than a century later, Christopher Smart was also confined in the same prison.

Francis, Christopher Smart's grandfather, married Margaret Gilpin of the family of Bernard Gilpin, the famous "Apostle of the North," a preacher during the reigns of Mary and Elizabeth, who distributed alms among the poor in Northumberland and Yorkshire. The poet's father, named Peter after the Puritan divine, was also intended for holy orders; instead, he became steward of the Fairlawn estate in Kent belonging to William, Viscount Vane, third son of the first Lord Barnard. The fine taste in literature of this Peter Smart was inherited by his son, according to Christopher Hunter, the poet's nephew and editor of *The Poems of the late Christopher Smart...* "to which is prefixed An Account of his Life and Writings" (Reading, 1791).

In 1720, when Peter Smart and his wife emigrated to Kent to assume his stewardship, they settled in the little village of Shipbourne. The parish records show a Margaret Ann born to the couple on October 11, 1720. No record is shown of Christopher Smart, but Hunter gives April

11, 1722, as the date of the poet's birth. Born prematurely, Smart was delicate as a child; his childhood days were spent not in the usual childish games but in study. Another effect of his delicate condition was his fondness of the cordials which were administered to him as tonic. Smart's later weakness for alcohol—a penchant which was to plague his whole life—has been attributed, in part, to his early drinking of liqueurs.

II   *Early Education and Life at Ruby Castle*

Young Kit, who had an alert and able mind, benefited greatly from his hours with his father's books and in his father's company. His precocity was demonstrated, according to Hunter, by a little poem Kit composed at the age of four. The poem was about a young lady of whom Smart was very fond, and a man who was a rival for her affections.

The poet's formal education started in the school in Maidstone, near Shipbourne. But a more far-reaching influence in his early education was his roaming of the Kentish countryside. His perceptive observation and keen appreciation of the bird and flower life about him—as well as other signs of nature—can be noted in his early *The Hop-Garden,* a poetic description of the Kentish hop-growing. His many references in the poem to the beauties of the natural setting, especially to the silver Medway River, illuminate these verses as they later glow in his more serious poetry, showing an astonishingly varied knowledge of the species of natural life. Even in his darkest hours, Smart remembered the meadows, brooks and hills of his early home.

In 1733, when Christopher Smart was a schoolboy eleven years of age, Peter Smart died. His widow left Kent, and Christopher and his two sisters were sent to Ruby Castle in Durham where they came under the protection of the Vane family. Hunter, in his biography of Smart prefixed to *Poems,* has noted that Mrs. Smart made this move because she believed her son would have the advantages of a good school at Durham and a change of air which would be beneficial to his health. In addition, Kit would have the help of his father's relatives.

Durham Grammar School, under Reverend Mr. Dongworth, was the school mentioned. There Smart made rapid progress. He began to develop a great interest in the Classics, an interest which brought reward in the poet's later life, being especially helpful in his career at

Cambridge. Smart had the highest affection and admiration for Reverend Mr. Dongworth, an old Etonion, who was a very fine teacher. On the occasion of the death of the educator in 1761, Smart wrote a petition for the blessing of the soul of Richard Dongworth.

An equally significant factor during the Durham period was the patronage of the Vane family at Ruby Castle, represented by Gilbert Vane, Lord Barnard, a descendant of the Sir Henry Vane who purchased Fairlawn early in the seventeenth century. Christopher and his two sisters, Margaret and Marianne, were often asked to the castle to play with the children of Lord Barnard, Henry and Anne Vane. Christopher was especially drawn to little Anne Vane. When the poet was about thirteen years old, he composed a poem for Anne: "To Ethelinda—on Her Doing My Verses the Honour of Wearing Them in Her Bosom." This ode inspired the two young lovers to plan a runaway match; fortunately, they were discovered and prevented from doing so.

Lady Anne later married the Honourable Charles Hope-Weir and, after a divorce, a George Monson; but Smart always had her in memory. In one of his poems dedicated to Lord Barnard, Smart wrote of "fair Ruby's towers," how awful and unforgettable, and of "Hope, copyist of her mother's mind . . . loveliest, liveliest of her kind." In *Jubilate Agno,* he described her in two notable and memorable lines:

> For I saw a blush in Staindrop Church, which was of
>   God's own colouring.
> For it was the benevolence of a virgin shewn to me
>   before the whole congregation (B_2, 668-69)

Smart was to remember his association with those at Ruby Castle for another reason. The grandmother of Anne Vane, the Duchess of Cleveland, was so impressed by Christopher's gifted nature that she granted him an annuity of forty pounds to see him through his university career.

III *Cambridge*

Christopher Smart left Staindrop to enter Pembroke College, Cambridge, on October 10, 1739, when he was seventeen years old. On the whole, his ten years at Cambridge were happy and successful. He emerged with friendships which were to be valuable to him later, a few years of teaching experience, and with some limited fame and experience as a writer. Although Smart had his annuity from the duchess, he was still obliged to work as a sizer—one who paid part of his fees by waiting on his Fellow Commoners, as had Edmund Spenser more than a century and a half earlier. The contrast between the lot of a sizer and that of the Fellow Commoners—most of whom had come to school mainly for support and excitement—must have seemed strange to Smart.

Unlike most of his fellow students, however, young Kit applied himself to his studies. His tutor, Leonard Addison, was one of the more conscientious of the university tutors. Smart's industry and scholastic promise—particularly his facility in writing Latin verses—brought him honors early in his college career. During his first year in college he was selected to write the Tripos Verses—a highly regarded achievement, which was repeated in 1741 and again in 1742.

An important milestone in Smart's academic career was his winning of the Craven scholarship in 1742 with a Latin translation of Pope's *Ode on Saint Cecilia's Day.* The stipend of twenty pounds, of course, was most welcome; but even more valuable was his resultant association with Pope, who wrote a courteous answer to Smart's proposal that he translate another of Pope's works, probably the *Essay on Man.* Pope thanked the young poet but suggested that perhaps a translation of his *Essay on Criticism* would be more agreeable both to the young writer and to his readers. There was further correspondence between the two, and Pope once received the young Cambridge student at Twickenham. Smart completed his translation of Pope's *Essay on Criticism,* but he did not published it until 1752, when he brought out a small edition of his poems.

The Pembroke Hall Jubilee, a celebration of the four-hundredth anniversary of the founding of the institution, was the occasion for another of Smart's poetic endeavors. For this celebration, probably held on New Year's Day, 1743-44, Smart wrote "A Secular Ode on the Jubilee at Pembroke Collee, Cambridge, in 1743." The poet afterward published this poem in *The Universal Visitor.* In January, 1744, Smart received his bachelor's degree, an event which he celebrated with another ode: "Ode on Taking a Bachelor's Degree," with allusion to Horace. With the attainment of this degree, the first period of Smart's academic career ended.

Smart's activities during the next year and a half can only be conjectured. He made several trips away from the college and may have been investigating the feasibility of pursuing a career in London. That he was doing a wide amount of reading is certain. The records of the college library show that Smart was interested in almost everything: philosophy, poetry, theology, science, and the Classics. He was storing away hundreds of bits of knowledge ultimately to be woven into the fabric of his poetry.

The first official academic recognition of Smart's studies was his appointment as a Fellow of Pembroke Hall, on July 5, 1745. Three months later, he was designated Praelector in Philosophy. At the same time he was chosen Keeper of the Common Chest—that is, treasurer—an office which brought him a welcome but small additional income. In the following year, he was reappointed to both posts, and in addition secured the appointment of Praelector of Rhetoric. As Praelector, Smart also served as tutor; a Pembroke College manuscript dated May 21, 1746, contains orders to tutors and shows Smart's as one of the appended signatures. Part of the instructions on the manuscript contains the note, "nine lectures every fortnight to each year by Mr. Smart."[2]

Smart continued to read widely and deeply. The record book of the Pembroke Library shows that in 1745 Smart read in Plato, Catullus, Tacitus, Lucian, Apollonius Rhodius, Pausanias, and Persius in the Classics. Among works of English literature, his reading included Pope's edition of Shakespeare, Beaumont and Fletcher, Thomas Fuller's *Worthies,* and an unidentified work on King David. This last work may have been Patrick Delany's *An Historical Account of the Life and Reign of David,* first published in London in 1740-42. Delany links David with the mythological Orpheus, a theme Smart used in his poem *On the Goodness of the Supreme Being.* Other religious works on his reading list included the Hebrew Bible, Whitby's *On the New Testament,* Henry Hammond's *New Testament,* Isaac Barrow's sermons, *The Lives of the Apostles,* and Erasmus.

The records for 1746-66 reveal Smart's further borrowings from the library: Homer and Strabo, and Locke's *Essay on Human Understanding.* His interest in philology can be seen in his numerous borrowings of *Graecae Linguae Theaurus* and the dictionaries of Jeremy Collier, Abel Bayer, and Ephraim Chambers. His readings in religious works continued with tracts such as Woolaston's *Religion and Nature,* Bishop Gilbert Burnet's *Pastoral Care,* and the sermons of Matthew

Newcome and Francis Atterbury. He continued to read in the Classics: Euripides, Sophocles, Aristophanes, Plutarch, and various Greek lyrists. The wide diversity of his reading is revealed in such selections as Aristotle's *Rhetoric*, Boethius's *Consolations of Philosophy*, Milton's *Defense of the English People*, Swift's *Tale of a Tub*, the letters of Roger Ascham, and Chaucer's poems. An indication of a love of flowers that continued all his life is shown by his borrowing of *Delphinium Planting*.

During this period Smart was doing a great deal of writing of a greatly varied kind. Many of these writings showed his Classical interests; others celebrated the beauties of girls he fancied himself in love with; some were of a humorous nature. One of his amorous poems links his tribute with another characteristic of the poet—his consciousness of being small. One of his odes is entitled "The Author Apologizes to a Lady for His being a Little Man" and describes Smart as an "amorous dwarf." He has also been spoken of as being black eyed and dapper.

Perhaps because of his consciousness of being small, Smart was very nervous and shy in company. Hunter relates how Smart, in later life, after introducing his wife to Lord Darlington, was so overcome by confusion that he became panic-stricken and retreated from the room, leaving his wife—in confusion—to follow him (p. xxix). Besides being shy, Smart was also sensitive and prone to take offense at imaginary slights. His writings at Cambridge demonstrate his sensitivity. On one occasion he even defended himself from anticipated criticism by pointing out in his preface to his own *Ode on St. Cecilia's Day* that he thought it unfair that anyone should criticize him for writing on the same subject as Pope's ode. Others writing on the same theme, he felt, were lucky to escape the kind of censure reserved for him.

Smart's sympathy and fundamental friendliness, however, overshadowed his shyness and sensitivity; for he made many friends at Cambridge. His affectionate nature and generosity made him always ready to lend a helping hand to a needy friend—often when he could ill afford such generosity. But his own friends were equally generous to him when his extravagance had brought him into debt. A letter written by Thomas Gray to his friend Thomas Warton in 1747 describes Smart as so deeply in debt that several of his friends had to sign his note to keep him from going to prison. Gray attributed the poet's predicament to his fondness for drink; Smart's drunkenness and extravagance were

such, indeed, that the Pembroke College authorities for a time refused
to reappoint him to his posts in 1747. The poet's confrontation with
his creditors, however, apparently had a sobering effect; for in the same
year he was granted a master's degree and began to do some serious
work. In 1748 he was reappointed to his old posts; he was apparently
again in good standing.

In 1748 Smart wrote a Pindaric *Ode to the King,* one of a number of
celebrations of the return of George II of England following the War of
the Austrian Succession. Smart's tribute, with similar ones, were
published in the *Gratulatio Academiae Cantabridiensis,* printed by the
university. Besides his writing for this collection, Smart was also making
an effort to get his own poetry published. A letter Smart wrote to a Mr.
Dodsley in London refers to the printing of proposals relating to a
collection of odes. No printing of these proposals occurred, however,
until two years later; and the collection did not appear until 1752.

The poet's life at Cambridge, however, was soon to be replaced by a
different kind of life—that of London. This move to England's great
city was one that Smart had contemplated for some time. The seclusion
of the university irked him; the literary center of eighteenth-century
England lay in London—the gathering place of the writers of the period.
Thus, shortly after the spring of 1749, Smart left Cambridge University
for London.

IV *London*

There is some difference of opinion among critics concerning
Smart's move to London—what the move suggested in terms of his
character and whether or not Smart's departure from academic life was
wise. Some critics consider the poet's move to London as the fatal step
downward toward the ruin of his career and prime evidence of the
weakness of will which led to drink and disaster. Other critics, however,
point to the aridity of the academic climate and to the literary vitality
of this period in London—the conversation in the coffee shops, the wit
and satire in the periodicals, the breadth of intellect and humanity in
the writers.

To those who feel that Smart did not make a mistake in going to
London—or that it did not indicate lack of willpower—Smart's move
demonstrated his capacity for decisive and difficult action. It was
surely, they point out, easier for Smart to stay on at Cambridge in a

safe, accustomed, known life than to brave the precarious one of a new writer in teeming London. Smart's departure for London did seem to show the seriousness with which he took his calling as a poet. And, while he probably did meet with some temptations there which increased his disposition to drink and helped to bring on his madness, he also gained from his association with the city's publishers and writers.

Smart did have one advantage in this venture—one provided by the authorities at Cambridge: he was allowed to retain his fellowship, and he received in addition certain sums in lieu of the board he would have received had he stayed on at the university. Although the authorities were obliged to withdraw his fellowship when his marriage in 1753 became known, they continued to keep his name on the books so that he could compete in an important religious-poem competition. The poet's eligibility for and success in this competition provided a continuing spark in the religious fervor which was to invest his greatest poem.

The literary scene of mid-eighteenth-century London was largely dominated by the booksellers, who were also the publishers of the period. Johnson had not yet emerged as a great literary figure, and most of the writers were poor and struggling. Authors were obliged to seek the booksellers, who were often printers as well as publishers, to dispose of their works. The writer had to sell his manuscript for the best price he could get, as the publisher had to assume all the risk.

But Christopher Smart had several advantages over his fellow writers. He had his remuneration from Cambridge and some poetry ready to offer for publication. In addition, he had made the acquaintance of a bookseller, John Newbery—one of the most important of the day. In June, 1750, Smart began to publish some of his material in a new magazine, *The Student, or the Oxford Monthly;* the name of this magazine was later changed to include the names of both Oxford and Cambridge universities. Smart continued to contribute to this magazine until it ceased publication; there is some foundation to the belief that he was the editor. In any event, he contributed substantially to it while waiting for subscriptions to his book of verse.

The writing of much varied material for *The Student* was well adapted to Smart's abilities. He had written in a variety of mediums— criticism, verse, exposition, and translation—and could glean from his wide reading to fill the pages of the magazine. His store of material written while at college also served to augment his current work. Smart's success at this early hackwork was achieved, perhaps, at a sacrifice, for his natural bent was toward the writing of more serious poetry and toward study and contemplation. The poet was able, however, to follow his natural bent in one instance: he competed for the Seatonian prize of thirty pounds and won it for his poem *On the Eternity of the Supreme Being.* Smart won this prize in the first year it was given (1750) and in every succeeding year in which he entered a poem for the competition.

But, as before noted, Smart could not spend much time on the religious poetry that he wrote with such fervor. A few months after Smart had begun working for *The Student,* he and Newbery collaborated on a new monthly magazine, *The Midwife* or *The Old Woman's Magazine,* which came out in October, 1750. Thus Smart was kept busy supplying both *The Student* and *The Midwife* with material under a variety of pseudonyms: "Mrs. Midnight," "Mary Midnight," "Mr. Lun," "Zosimus Zepher," "Ebenezer Pentweazle," and many others. As a result, scholars have had much difficulty in identifying the products of Smart's pen.

"Mary Midnight," or "Mrs. Midnight," however, was the most common name under which Smart—and possibly Newbery, Richard Rolt, and Bonnell Thorton—wrote in *The Midwife.* Mrs. Midnight, a lady of wide interests, is described in a selection from *The Midwife* as being a traveler who "came to London, fraught with learning and experience, and frequented the coffee-houses and other places about town, where the sage and polite resort, dressed in a high crown hat, and otherwise accoutred like a piece of venerable antiquity."[3] Through this creation came a barrage of comment: Mrs. Midnight's views on foreign affairs, her accounts of rambles through the poor district of London, notes concerning curious discoveries in England, and predictions about the fate of the country in the distant future. She also established a correspondence with various readers whom she advised on subjects such as marriage, concerning which she gave not only her own but the opinion of great thinkers such as Socrates, Solomon, and Sir Thomas More.

Probably some of the original Greek and Latin verse in *The Midwife* was also Smart's, for the magazine was intended to appeal to a wide range of readers. The poet also used its pages to puff his own poetry as well as the work of his friends and of people he admired. One of the

writers he praised most effusively was Samuel Johnson, who contributed one essay—reprinted from *The Rambler*—to each number of *The
Midwife.* Other writers Smart mentioned favorably included William
Collins, Lord Chesterfield, and Henry Fielding. Smart, in addition to his
other work, published a volume of jests called *The Nutcracker* (1750).

In the early part of 1751, Smart became involved in one of the
literary fights so prevalent during the period. A hack writer named
William Kenrick had written in a derogatory fashion about *The Midwife.*
Smart announced his intention of denouncing Kenrick in *The
Midwife.* Before Smart could publish his satire, however, Kenrick
brought forth an *Old Woman's Dunciad* of his own, satirizing Smart and
purporting to be from the press of *The Midwife.*

But in March, 1751, an opportunity occurred for Smart which was
designed to soothe his injured feelings—a chance to be once more
associated with the aristocratic Delavals. John Blake Delaval, Smart's
former student at Cambridge, asked the poet to write an epilogue and
prologue to an amateur performance of *Othello.* The performance was
given before a notable company of guests, including the Prince and
Princess of Wales; and Smart praised it highly in *The Midwife.* He also
printed his epilogue and prologue in *The Midwife,* with complimentary
comment.

The success of this theatrical venture led Smart and Newbery to try
to bolster the circulation of *The Midwife* with a Mary-Midnight
entertainment. Smart called his show *The Old Woman's Oratory* or
Henley in Petticoats, and he may have played Mary Midnight himself.
This show, with a variety of music-hall stunts, proved so popular that
Smart began to spend the greater portion of his time in its
production—to the detriment of *The Midwife.* The magazine began to
be issued only sporadically, and finally it ceased publication in 1753.

V *Early Publication of Poetry*

Smart had meanwhile made some serious efforts toward the
publication of more serious verse. He composed a "Dirge" upon the
death of the Prince of Wales and again won the Seatonian prize. His
greatest achievement of the period, however, was the edition *Poems on
Several Occasions* published by Newbery in June, 1752. This volume
was quite a literary success; more than seven hundred subscribers
guaranteed it to be a fruitful financial venture. Among these subscribers

were such famous people as Voltaire and Samuel Richardson, the novelist. Smart's old acquaintance from Cambridge, Thomas Gray, was also a subscriber. Smart's early drudgery at literary hackwork in *The Student* seemed justified with the appearance of this volume of poems.

One of the reviews of *Poems on Several Occasions,* a discussion by a "Sir" John Hill—with whom Smart had had several skirmishes before—especially aroused the poet's ire. Hill, who called Smart a "bold borrower," suggested that the contents of the *Poems* did not justify the price. After several exchanges between the two writers, Smart determined to attack Hill in a satiric Dunciad-like piece. Calling his own mock-epic a product of his desire for justice, not revenge, Smart brought out his *Hilliad* early in 1753. Newbery accompanied its publication with two introductory letters: one from Smart to a fellow poet—possibly Gray—decried the literary criticism of the period and named Hill as a chief offender; the other, written by Arthur Hill, urged Smart to aid the deplorable condition of English letters by demolishing John Hill. Smart abandoned the quarrel after his *Hilliad,* but several of his enemies wrote retaliatory pieces.

VI *Smart's Marriage*

Smart had written a number of poems celebrating the beauties of ladies whom he admired, but an ode entitled "The Lass with the Golden Locks"—concerning Anna-Maria Carnan—seemed to mark the end of his philandering. Smart met Anna-Maria through his association with Newbery, her stepfather; and by the close of 1751 Smart had proclaimed through the "Lass": "No more of my Harriot, of Polly no more. Nor all the bright beauties that charm'd me before."

There is some dispute as to the exact date of his marriage. In January, 1752, Smart wrote a poem in honor of her birthday in which he says, "I long to see the blooming Maid/ Chang'd to the blushing Bride." After an illness of the poet during which he was nursed back to health by Miss Carnan, he wrote that "joined to her, O May I prove/ By friendship, gratitude and love/ The poverty of wealth," which seems to indicate that he was already married or was contemplating it very shortly. The year 1753—the one generally assigned to the marriage of Smart—seems too late; Mrs. Smart herself told her daughters that she was married in 1752. It can reasonably be thought that Mrs. Smart's declaration was true and that the marriage was kept a secret so that Smart could go on receiving money from his Pembroke fellowship.

Their first child, Marianne, named after Smart's younger sister, was born on May 3, 1753; she is the "Polly" of Smart's later poems, whom some biographers have wrongly identified with the former sweetheart mentioned in "No more of my Harriot, of Polly no more." On October 27, 1754, their second daughter, Elizabeth Anne (Bess), was born. This second daughter recorded for posterity valuable knowledge of her father and his work.

Although Smart had not notified the college authorities of his wedding, the affair in the meantime had come to the attention of the university. On November 27, 1753, an entry was made in the Pembroke books ordering the dividend assigned to Mr. Smart to be held in the treasury until a rumor that he was married be proved or disproved. The dividend was stopped, but the authorities allowed Smart to keep his name on the books free of charge as long as he continued to submit an entry for the Seatonian prize. This decision was advantageous not only to the poet, who was thus allowed to compete for the fame and money of the Seatonian premium, but also to Pembroke because of the added prestige such a victory gave the college.

Another reason for the clandestine nature of Smart's marriage may have been a religious one. Anna-Maria was Catholic, and the marriage ceremony and the baptism of Marianne were probably both Catholic, but no records of these two services can be found. Smart probably allowed his first daughter to be reared in her mother's faith, following the example of Mr. Newbery, who allowed his wife to rear their own daughter in the Catholic faith although he was not Catholic. Smart's second daughter, Elizabeth Anne, however, was brought up in the faith of the Church of England—an indication of a change in Smart's attitudes.

This change of religious attitude on the part of Smart was an important one and was reflected in his later madness. He later noted in the *Jubilate Agno* that he had married a "Moabitish" woman ("Moabite" being the traditional Puritan name for Roman Catholic), and that Polly, his eldest daughter, had been alienated from the house of David (the Church of England). This observation was a part of the poet's larger obsession that he was a kind of prophet bringing all faiths into a Catholic and Universal Church of England.

But there is little evidence of this mania in the first few years of the Smart marriage. The poet brought his bride to Canonbury House in Islington, where both of Smart's daughters were born. Canonbury House had once been a hunting lodge and the seat in 1593 of Sir John

Spencer, Lord Mayor. In the 1750's it had become a lodging house. Besides Goldsmith, the Newberys, and the Smarts, Samuel Humphrey and Ephraim Chambers lived there. Smart's old enemy, John Hill, died while in residence there.

Mrs. Smart seems to have been quietly attractive, pious, capable, kindhearted, and well read. She won the devotion of her daughters and her stepfather, Newbery, as well as that of her sisters-in-law, Smart's sisters; Dr. Johnson admired her deeply. That she had to put up with many of Smart's less admirable qualities there is little doubt. Smart often invited company to dinner when there was no means of providing a meal for the family itself.

Another problem in their marriage was Smart's drunkenness, which has been variously viewed by critics. Some paint a dark and unhappy picture of a home riddled by debt, poverty, and Smart's drunkenness, pointing to Hunter's reference to the poet's "deviations from the rules of sobriety."[4] Others who note the enormous production of writing in the period after Smart first came to London, suggest that—while Smart was fond of drinking as far back as his Cambridge days—he was not a vicious drunkard; he was merely a merry, social drinker. Kenrick, in his *Pasquinade* of January, 1753, suggests this last view of Smart: "With Cyder muddled, or inspired with Bub,/ In Newbery's Garrett, or in Heley's Tub,/ For Mugs of Porter pun and crack his jokes."[5] One of the damaging pieces of evidence concerning the poet's drinking is Dr. Johnson's remark: "He used, before his confinement, to walk to the ale-house for exercise, but he was carried back."[6]

Despite the clouds that seem to hang over Smart's residence in Canonbury House, he appears to have had happy recollections of his stay there. In *Jubilate Agno* he wrote: "For I bless God for my retreat at Canbury, as it was the place of the nativity of my children" (B_1, 75).

VII   *Last Writings Before Confinement*

In the first part of 1753, Smart seemed quite busy and had at least a fair means of support from his writing. He had always had a fondness for fables—one or two were included in his 1752 volume of collected poems—and during this year he worked on a collection of eighteen fables in verse. Several were published in the *Gentleman's Magazine*, but most of them were reserved for a later volume of poems. Modeled on

John Gay's witty fables of a quarter-century earlier, Smart's verses are somewhat more fanciful and thoughtful; but they suffer in comparison with Gay's.

Beginning with the February, 1754, issue of the *Gentleman's Magazine*, Smart became a regular contributor to its poetry section. In addition to the few fables noted earlier, he printed a number of other poems, including several odes and a paraphrase of the Lord's Prayer. Several of these pieces may have been writings that Smart had done before because he does include some reprints of material submitted to the *Gentleman's Magazine*. Smart did not submit an entry for the Seatonian prize in 1754; his failure to enter a poem for this competition and his use of old material suggests that he may not have been well during the last part of the year.

Smart submitted a few poems to the *Gentleman's Magazine* in 1755: "Mrs. Abigail and the Dumb Waiter," and "Lady Harriot," in February; "The Country Squire" and "The Mandrake" in April. "Epitaph on Mrs. Rolt," appearing in the June issue, may also be Smart's; an epilogue, "Who'er begot these had no cause to blush," appeared in the December issue. He submitted an entry for the Seatonian prize this year, but was so late in writing it that he barely had time to rush it to Cambridge in time for the judges to consider it; this poem, *On the Goodness of the Supreme Being,* again won the prize.

Although the sparsity of publications seems to indicate idleness on Smart's part, the fact was that he was working on a project which he detested but which he felt obliged to undertake to support his family: a translation in prose of the complete works of Horace that was to be published by Newbery. Smart much preferred to make this translation in verse, but he could not take the time for such a demanding project because he needed the money. In his preface to his prose translation Smart apologizes for offering such a piece of hackwork to the public—especially from himself, whom he characterizes as a person who had made poetry too much, perhaps, the business of his life. He suggests, however, that the translation may be useful to those wishing to acquire or to recover a knowledge of Latin. He hopes, in conclusion, that his "labour" has not been in vain. For such a work, he reiterates, is pure *"labour"*—if a man had any pretensions of genius, he would not have used it in such a way.

This translation, published in 1756, was a great financial success.

Smart, however, received only thirteen pounds of the original one hundred promised by Newbery. The rest of the commission was given by Newbery to Smart's family. The poet was deeply resentful of Newbery's action, even though the money was no doubt used to better advantage in this way than if the entire amount had been given to Smart. The work itself went into a number of editions and was used by schoolboys—among them Robert Browning—for many years.

Offended as Smart was by Newbery's interference in his affairs, Smart at this time seems to have been contemplating a new publication: his fables in verse. In the first volume of his translation of Horace, Smart had promised that such a volume would "speedily" be produced and that it would appeal to people of all ranks. Newbery also advertised the coming appearance of this work, but Smart did not proceed with his volume. Instead, he turned, perhaps partly from a desire to sever connections with Newbery and partly from a hope of better and speedier profits, to a new periodical venture: *The Universal Visitor.*

The material for *The Universal Visitor* was to be supplied by Smart and Richard Rolt to a bookseller, Thomas Gardner, under a contract concerning which there were some conflicting opinions. The terms of the contract were these: Smart and Rolt, who were to write for no other periodical for a period of ninety-nine years, were to share one-third of the profits. Johnson called this stipulation an example of "the oppression of booksellers toward poor authors."[7] Boswell pointed out, however, that Johnson had misunderstood the terms. Smart and Rolt were to be allowed to publish any other material they wished, but they were not to write for any other periodical. And materials and pamphlets by Rolt and Smart did appear while the contract was in force. A further condition made the contract even more fair: if the enterprise lost money within any six-month period, any signer might give notice and free himself from obligation.

The first number of *The Universal Visitor* appeared on February 2, 1756, but was succeeded by only eleven other issues. Smart was able to contribute little to it, as his mind was giving way. Several of the poems he submitted were reprints from *The Student* and *The Midwife.* A new ode, "Ode to the Earl of Darlington," was first printed in *The Visitor;* and Smart reprinted another ode from his Cambridge days. Although the poet's friends—among them Samuel Johnson—contributed material to *The Visitor* with hopes that Smart would finally recover his sanity, the magazine had to cease publication. For this year marked the beginning of Smart's unhappy seven years of madness.

VIII   *Smart's Madness*

Although there is some difference of opinion concerning the progress of Smart's illness, there appear to be some times during the period when Smart tried to return to normal life; others, when he was confined in various places. In the early stages of his insanity he seems to have been confined in the first month of 1756 to the home of Newbery. The hope that his obsession would be only temporary explains, of course, the efforts of Smart's friends to continue to supply *The Visitor* with material, as has been noted. Accompanying this kind practicality on the part of the poet's friends was perhaps also a reluctance to disavow entirely a madness so religiously oriented.

For Smart's madness consisted of his efforts to obey literally St. Paul's injunction to the Thessalonians: "Pray without ceasing." The poet may have been influenced, some critics feel, by reading William Law's *The Spirit of Prayer; or The Soul Rising out of the Vanity of Time, into the Riches of Eternity,* a book which suggests that life can—if man so wills it—be a continual state of prayer toward God; that without prayer, man continually separates himself from God. Beginning with private prayer, Smart abandoned himself to praying whenever the spirit to do so moved him—no matter where he was; and he urged anyone with him to follow. Dr. Johnson commented thus on Smart's illness: "My poor friend Smart shewed the disturbance of his mind, by falling upon his knees, and saying his prayers in the street, or in any other unusual place. Now although, rationally speaking, it is greater madness not to pray at all, than to pray as Smart did, I am afraid there are so many who do not pray, that their understanding is not called in question." An even more famous comment by Johnson concerning the question of Smart's obsession is the following: "I do not think he ought to be shut up. His infirmities are not noxious to society. He insisted on people praying with him; and I'd as lief pray with Kit Smart as any one else. Another charge was that he did not love clean linen; and I have no passion for it."[8]

Others did not share Johnson's kind tolerance of Smart's deviation, and his behavior did, in fact, finally become more than an embarrassment. Smart called his friends away from dinner, from their beds, and from entertainments either to pray with him or to join him in the streets in praise of God. The poet himself wrote later in *Jubilate Agno* that he "routed" the company in St. James's Park with his praying, and that "the officers of the peace are at variance with me, and the watchman smites me with his staff"(B1, 90).

Smart did make, however, a brief recovery from his first illness of the year and celebrated with *Hymn to the Supreme Being, on Recovery from a dangerous Fit of Illness,* published in 1756. His greatest rejoicing, however, was with a spiritual rebirth he felt he had undergone. In his *Hymn* he affirms that his eyes will henceforth be "heaven-directed"; no more with "Deeds, thoughts, and words" will he break Christ's mandates, "But to his endless glory work, conceive, and speak." Like King Hezekiah, whose story formed the theme of the poem, Smart felt himself restored to life while at the point of death so that he might devote his talents solely to God. The *Hymn,* while actually written in gratitude to Dr. James and his fever-powders for curing Smart's sickness, does display the poet's new firmness and determined attitude toward his work: he will not prostrate his genius to unworthy activity, but to the highest of conceptions.

While Smart had probably suffered some periods of delirium during his early illness in 1756, he now—in his determination to make his life a prayer and testimony to God—displayed the symptoms mentioned in Johnson's comment on his illness. Yet he appeared to know what he was doing. What made his condition all the more distressing to his friends and relatives was Smart's seeming resemblance to certain relatively uneducated and highly emotional prophets who were preaching their private revelations to the London crowd. Methodists, in particular, were addicted to public prayer with what was thought to be overly charged high spirits. Such displayers of religious emotionalism were often confined not only to private madhouses, but also to Bedlam—a situation that was a potential danger to Smart.

The fact that his wife was a Roman Catholic added another perilous element to Smart's problem. A Roman Catholic was also a Bedlamite figure: William Hogarth in his painting of the horrors of Bedlam depicts a Roman Catholic praying to his images. Papists were therefore included with Methodists as being disturbers of the Kingdom of God. Although many broad-minded men disapproved of this intolerance, most of the laws against the Catholics were still on the books— disregarded for the most part unless a specific case was noticeable. Smart's public demonstrations, then, could have drawn attention to the whole household and have placed Smart's wife and her mother in danger. Thus in June, 1756, Smart, with the consent of his relatives, was put in confinement by Newbery and Carnan.

For a little less than a year, Smart was confined in a private asylum, writing very little and praying constantly. During the year of 1756, Newbery published the first edition of *On the Goodness of the Supreme Being,* the third editions of *The Eternity* and *The Immensity* essays, the second edition of *The Omniscience* essay, and the *Hymn to the Supreme Being.* In 1757 he published a compilation of essays from *The Midwife,* the *Nonpareil,* the *Index of Mankind.* Another edition of *On the Power of the Supreme Being* was issued in 1758.

Smart's family had reason to be grateful for Newbery's kindness in publishing the poet's work; for the poet's disorder growing worse, he was finally sent to St. Luke's Hospital in May, 1757. Here he came under the supervision of a Dr. William Battie, who had more humanitarian views of the treatment of the insane than was prevalent at Bedlam. Not only were patients exempt from many of the harsh methods of Bedlam, but visits of sightseers to the madhouse—a great eighteenth-century pastime—were also forbidden. Since Battie also refused to allow any relatives and friends of the confined patient to visit and perhaps disturb him, Smart may not have seen even his wife and children during this period.

On May 12, 1758, Christopher Smart left St. Luke's, discharged as "incurable." As an "incurable," he could be readmitted when there was a vacancy; his name, then, was kept on a waiting list. He may have gone back to Dr. Battie's private house for a few months. Hunter has described Smart as "pretty well restored"(p. xxii), but this conjecture was probably the result of the poet's learning to control severely any outward showing of his impulse to indulge in public prayer and the like. Inwardly, he does not appear to have changed; he still regarded himself as an emissary of God chosen for a special purpose. Battie probably pronounced him incurable because his patient's obsession had not disappeared.

Although Smart was released earlier, he does not seem to have appeared on the London scene much before January, 1759, when his friends began to help him reestablish himself. His friend David Garrick presented for Smart's benefit a twin bill: *Mérope,* an adaptation of Voltaire's *Mérope,* and *The Guardian,* adapted by Garrick from Christophe-Barthelemy Fagan's *La Pupille.* The performance was given at Drury Lane on February 3, 1759. Previously the bill had been announced in *The Public Advertiser* of January 17, 1759, as being "For the Benefit of a Gentleman, well known in the Literary World, who is at present under very unhappy circumstances."[9]

The affair was a great success; his friends did their best, both in *The Advertiser* and in other ways, to make the performance known to the public. Some of the tributes are valuable evidence not only of the great affection that the poet generated—which the generous and eager aid given to him had already demonstrated—but of the admiration they had for him as a poet and as a man. Arthur Murphy, in a tribute in *The Advertiser,* praised several of Smart's poems and then spoke of the poet's benevolence, his public spirit, his steadfast morals, and his genius. But Murphy suggested that Smart might not be able to write again, a fear echoed by some of Smart's other friends. Gray wrote a letter to a friend, William Mason, to the effect that he had seen the announcement of the benefit in the *Advertiser* and was surprised; he had thought Smart dead. Mason replied that Smart would probably be better off if he were dead.

Despite the gloomy observation of his friends, however, Smart seemed to have made his way fairly well in the first six months of 1759 while staying at his former bachelor quarters in St. James's Park. His wife and children were not living in England at the time: they had left for Ireland the previous year. Anna-Maria, as shown by advertisements appearing in the *London Gazeteer* of the period, had established herself in Dublin where, as an agent for Newbery, she sold Dr. James's powders. She seemed to have made her residence with her husband's sister and brother-in-law, Richard Falkiner, a barrister. Johnson wrote her several letters, one of which asks her to send him the particulars of her business venture, her home, and her companions.

Mrs. Smart stayed in Dublin for some time. In 1761 Smart's Seaton poems were republished, but it is not certain that she had anything to do with the reissue. By 1762 she was back in Reading, taking over the publication of her father's newspaper, the *Oxford Gazette and Reading Mercury.* A January 25 issue bears a notation indicating that the journal was printed for Anna-Maria Smart and company. She outlived her husband by thirty-eight years, leading a successful life as a woman of business and a worthy life as a Roman Catholic. Her daughters retained an interest in the publishing business. Marianne continued to publish the *Mercury,* an enterprise carried on by her descendants until recent years. Elizabeth, who married a French émigré, a Captain Le Noir, continued in a small way her father's literary pursuits by publishing a novel and poems in the early nineteenth century.

It is difficult to determine accurately Smart's family's attitude toward him during his periods of confinement. The poet himself did not indicate any sense of missing his family for some time; he seemed intent on his dream. Certainly during 1759 he was starting to write his *Jubilate Agno,* a kind of poetic diary about his days in the asylum. This manuscript, which has a number of biographical references, partially reveals what happened to Smart from the time of Garrick's benefit until *A Song to David.* There seems to be an indication, for example, that he was out of the asylum, then readmitted in the late summer of 1759. In *Jubilate* he expressed his dedication to God and a willingness to make any sacrifice to advance his mission as he conceived it.

Toward the close of Smart's confinement—within the last year or two of his final period in the asylum—Smart began a new poetic enterprise, but he still kept a running account of his concerns in *Jubilate Agno.* His new venture was a translation of the Psalms into rhyming verse; he also composed a completely new set of hymns for every feast day of the Church of England, a project long contemplated. He may also have worked on some of his later poems because he became particularly concerned during this period of his confinement with the technique of verse; his individual style developed during this time.

IX *Release*

It is difficult to establish the exact date of Smart's release from the asylum. The last date marked in *Jubilate Agno* was "New Year by Old Stile 1763"—January 11; and he was probably confined when he wrote that entry. Shortly afterward he was released as a result of the efforts of his friend, John Sherratt, whose help the poet celebrated in "Epistle to John Sherratt," published in June or July of 1763. How Sherratt was able to effect Smart's release is not known, but there was an inquiry at the time into abuses in the reception and retention of persons in private madhouses. Sherratt, who may simply have removed Smart, may have been allowed to do so because of the uneasy feelings of the authorities of the asylum.

Smart seems to have reentered the world with renewed hope and enthusiasm, and his friends rallied to help him in any way they could. In the last part of January, 1763, there appeared *Mrs. Midnight's Orations,* a collection of pieces used in the performances; this volume, published by Richard Rolt, was probably a means of securing needed funds for the poet. Smart himself set about getting subscribers for his translation of the Psalms. He was especially anxious to have his work published as soon as possible because of a rival version by James Merrick, which was to be published by Newbery. Smart's volume finally appeared in 1765.

Despite the promise of a rival edition, the list of subscribers to Smart's translation was impressive; there were over seven hundred names of his friends and admirers. Although the poet's wife's name was not listed—as perhaps need not have been expected—Marianne and her Irish husband, as well as his sister Margaret and her husband Dr. Hunter, appeared on the list. Other subscribers included some of the nobility, among them the Earl of Darlington and several Vanes and Delavals; John Wilkes and Charles Churchill, who may have helped with his release. The names of a great number of his old London friends also appeared: Arthur Murphy, Garrick, Hogarth, the Tyers family, Charles Burney, and Dr. Thomas Arne. Others included William Cowper, Thomas and Joseph Wharton, Tobias Smollett, Mark Adenside, and Richard Cumberland. Even the name of William Kenrick—Smart's old combatant—appeared. A listing of the personages to whom Smart had devoted poems includes the Sheeles family, John Sheratt, Reverend Mr. Tyler, and Brigadier-General William Draper—a hero of Smart's—who put his name down for forty copies. Smart's old Cambridge friends proved faithful: Boyce, Randall, Thomas Gray, Mason, Stonhuer, and Addison.

A notable exception—considering his kindness toward and interest in Smart—was the name of Dr. Johnson. This hard-to-explain omission does not appear to be the result of a quarrel. The names of Newbery and Carnan also failed to appear, but this failure was probably the consequence of their commitment to publish a rival translation. In addition, Newbery might have felt that Smart still held some animosity toward him because of his withholding part of the poet's fee for translating Horace. But Smart's quarrels with his family and his efforts to secure subscribers to his translation were superseded—in the eyes of posterity, if not those of the eighteenth century—by the appearance of his great masterpiece, *A Song to David.*

X   *Publications after Release from the Asylum*

On April 8, 1763, a few months after his release from the asylum, Smart's *A Song to David* was published by Fletcher of the Oxford Theatre in St. Paul's Courtyard. The price was one shilling, and every copy was signed by the writer. At the close of the poem, Smart advertised his subscription for *A Translation of the Psalms of David* and *A Set of Hymns for the Fasts and Festivals of the Church of England.* Both the poet's work on the *Jubilate* and *A Translation of the Psalms* had helped prepare him for the great piece of writing, *A Song to David.* He had a treasure of phrases, images, and rhymes from which to draw to enhance the fabric of his masterpiece. But *A Song to David* owed only part of its glory to the poet's previous work on the *Psalms,* for Smart drew not only from other parts of the Bible but from his deep reading and poetic knowledge.

The literary world of the eighteenth century granted *A Song to David* an unfavorable reception. A few critics and commentators on the literary scene gave it a little qualified praise—Boswell called it "a very curious composition, being a strange mixture of *dun obscure* and glowing genius at times."[10] But the poem was probably too exotic and unorthodox for contemporary taste. Perhaps the London commentators, who could not forget Smart's recent confinement, concluded that the product of a mad poet could not be worth much.

Although Smart was no doubt very much distressed about the poor reception accorded *A Song to David,* he was also embroiled in plans for a lawsuit. Mason, in a letter of June, 1763, mentions his concern over what to do with money he was collecting for the subscriptions to Smart's *Psalms.* Considering the news in the paper that Smart was planning to prosecute the people who had confined him, observed Mason, the money collected—if given to Smart—would only aid his lawyers. Some biographers believe Mason's statement about the suit refers to Newbery and Carnan; Devlin, however, points to Smart's references to "adversaries" (responsible for his second confinement) in *Jubilate* as intended for Francis Smart and Richard Smart, who seem to have had something to do with Smart's exclusion from inheriting Staindrop Moor, the ancestral home (Smart was heir-at-law). Gray, who replied to Mason's letter in July, 1763, advised Mason to hold any collected money until Smart had dropped his suit, which he feared would go against the poet if he pursued it. Smart was evidently persuaded to forgo legal action, as no evidence of it is in on record.

In spite of his contemplated legal action, Smart was working hard to get his work published; but he was still having trouble with his critics. A pamphlet collection of poems, including *Reason and Imagination,* appeared in July, 1763. In the advertisement of this volume, Smart bitterly denounced the comments of the *Critical Review* concerning *A Song to David.* The critical remarks about *A Song,* exclaimed Smart, revealed both the commentators' lack of religion and their poverty of learning. The July *Critical Review* contained a satirical retort to Smart's accusation, and the *Monthly Review* entered the fray with an insulting review of Smart's poems in the *Reason and Imagination* pamphlet.

Another volume of Smart's verse, *Poems on Several Occasions,* including *Munificence and Modesty,* published in Novembers, 1763, contained the poet's reply to the *Monthly's* remarks. This time Smart enumerated offenses he felt done him from the time of John Hill's review of the 1752 *Poems on Several Occasions.* Again the *Monthly,* in its review of *Munificence and Modesty,* gave a not unjustified answer: Smart's resentment would prevent the publication from making in the future any critical remarks at all about his writing. To antagonize these two critical magazines was a major error on Smart's part. He should have patched up his quarrel with the periodicals, just as he had buried his resentment of Kenrick. As a result of the feud between the poet and commentators, very little comment concerning Smart's work appeared in publications; and what was published tended to be derogatory.

Smart was writing very industriously now, with fairly frequent publication. In April, 1764, he published an oratorio, *Hannah,* with music written by the same Morgan who had composed for his *Solemn Dirge* twelve years before. But this oratorio was no *Mother Midnight's Entertainment* or popular cantata for the Vauxhall Gardens. *Hannah* was in keeping with Smart's determined literary bent and his steadfast religious feeling. Performed at the King's Theatre in the Haymarket on April 3, *Hannah* seems to have caused little stir. The printed version, according to the *St. James* magazine of May, had some poetical merit.

In July, 1764, a new pamphlet collection of poems entitled *Ode to the Earl of Northumberland. . .With some other pieces* was published by Dodsley. Besides the several odes to his aristocratic friends, Smart also included some charming short lyrics. This work met with some adverse criticism, but *The Public Advertiser,* which had somewhat kindlier comment, spoke of the poet's spontaneity and genuine feeling for his subject.

Smart's last publication in 1764 was *A Poetical Translation of the Fables of Phaedrus,* advertised in *The Public Advertiser* on December of that year. This quite ambitious work printed the original Latin and the translation on opposite pages, and included a parsing index for students. Smart dedicated this volume to young Master J. H. Delaval with a note of thanks for the favors given him by Master Delaval's parents. *Phaedrus,* too, won varied critical comment, but this translation did not prove as popular as Smart's earlier one of Horace. It was, however, reprinted without the original in 1831, and again in 1853. While the original publication, commissioned by Dodsley now that the poet had broken with Newbery, did nothing to enhance Smart's literary reputation, it did supply him with some badly needed money.

The long-proposed edition of the translated Psalms was beset with difficulties. The original printer, Charles Say, scared by the poor sale of *A Song to David,* had backed out, and no other printer seemed inclined to take the new risk. Some of the money advanced by the subscribers may have vanished. But, as usual, Smart's loyal friends did not desert him. Those associated with music sponsored a collection of forty-five songs by twelve well-known organists, such as William Boyce. These melodies, corresponding to the different verse forms used in Smart's translation, met a good reception. Encouraged by the belief that such a version would be used in church services and so result in a good sale, the distinguished printer Dryden Leach agreed to accept the work.

An interesting sidelight on Smart's activities and attitudes toward the end of 1764 is revealed in a letter dated October. The letter is from a Dr. John Hawkesworth, a close friend of Charles Burney and also a friend of Smart's mother and sisters. Dr. Hawkesworth had been asked by the poet's mother and sister to visit Smart in London and find out how things stood, for the poet had divorced himself from his own family as well as from his wife. In this letter to Smart's sister, Mrs. Hunter, Hawkesworth relates the joy and friendliness with which the poet greeted his visitor. When the doctor mentioned his trip to Margate, his having seen the poet's sister and his mother, and their concern for him, Smart did not ask about his mother and sister nor about the place, or about why Hawkesworth had come to see him. After a little while, Hawkesworth returned to the subject and mentioned that Mr. and Mrs. Hunter would be very glad to see him at Margate. Smart quickly replied, "I cannot afford to be idle."[11] When Hawkesworth suggested that the poet might also work in the country, as well as in town, Smart only shook his head and changed the subject.

Then they went on to other topics, and the poet told Hawkesworth about some of his undertakings: his translation of *Phaedrus,* the coming publication of his Psalms, and of his translation of Horace into verse. When the prose translation of Horace was mentioned, Smart, who became really disturbed, accused Newbery of having given him only thirteen pounds for the translation. His visitor shared Smart's excitement until he discovered that the total payment from the work was one hundred pounds. Realizing the poet's resentment over the matter, Hawkesworth quickly changed the subject. The letter writer then describes the pleasantness not only of Smart's lodging overlooking St. James's Park but of his social life with various eminent people of the city. The poet was to dine that night with a Mr. Richard Dalton, who had an appointment in the king's library; and Smart had lately received a very "genteel" letter from Dr. Robert Lowth.

The critic Christopher Devlin, in *Poor Kit Smart,* believes that the foregoing letter belies the impression conveyed by some writers that the poet was a habitual drunkard; Devlin quotes Hawkesworth's own words concerning Smart: the poet was not considered in any light that made his company as a scholar, a gentleman, and a genius less desirable. Devlin further susbstantiates this claim by quoting two lines from Smart's verse-epistle to Dr. Nares, the musician—the poet often wrote invitations or thanks in verse—which ends: "P.S. I have (don't think it a chimaera) /Some good sound Port and right Madeira." Smart could not have written about drink in this casual and friendly way, thinks Devlin, if he had been a drunkard.

Other evidence supporting Hawkesworth's remarks about Smart's acceptability occurs in an account by a John Kempe, who died June 1, 1823, at the age of seventy-five. John Kempe had resided for some time, according to the account, at the home of his father, who had entertained many eminent people during his day. Among those mentioned were George Romney, the portrait painter; Sir Thomas Robinson; "the unhappy poet Smart"; and Mrs. N. Kempe's sister,

Lady Hamer. John Kempe is quoted as saying that "Smart loved to hear me play upon my flute, and I have often soothed the wanderings of his melancholy by some favorite air; he would shed tears when I played, and generally wrote some lines afterwards."[12]

Smart was discouraged; for, in spite of his beginning to make efforts toward the publication of his translation of the Psalms as soon as he left the asylum and his enlisting many of his wide circle of acquaintances as subscribers, the long-awaited volume did not appear until August, 1765. In the meantime, Merrick's translation, published by Newbery, a work Smart had hoped to precede with his own, was already on the market. There were inevitable comparisons between the two translations; Smart's, partly because of his quarrel with some of the leading periodicals and partly because its appearance was anticlimatic, came off second best. The *Monthly's* brief comment was that, since Smart's writings had seemed to be exempt from criticism, the publication would be silent in regard to the merit of his present work. The *Critical,* less direct but more derogatory, spoke of the deliverance of the Psalmist from wretched poets who "had overwhelmed his native grace and dignity under the rubbish of their despicable schemes."[13] If one wanted to read a beautiful translation of the Psalms, the *Critical* suggested Merrick's translation.

The majority of literary London seemed to agree with the *Critical's* judgment, as did the religious authorities. Merrick's translations were extensively used by the Church of England and by the Nonconformists in the early part of the nineteenth century; his hymn, "The Festal Morn, O God, is come," is still sung in Congregational churches. No hymn by Smart appears in any hymn book or prayer book, although his daughter Elizabeth did include a few in the volume of her own poems issued in 1826.

Thus, one of Smart's dearest hopes—the acceptance of his work by the Church of England—was frustrated. This refusal of the Church to acknowledge him was a far greater blow to Smart than the critical comments of the periodicals. Although Dr. Lowth—the author of a book on Hebrew poetry which influenced Smart, and a man who had spoken favorably of the poet—was given his bishopric at St. David's in 1766, he did not further aid the poet. Neither the official Anglican or the progressive—later Evangelical—element of the religious groups favored Smart; they thought the poet too popish.

Smart, who was a Mason, may also have been aided by his lodge brothers. Smart mentions his being a builder and a "free and accepted Mason" in *Jubilate Agno.* A pamphlet of the day, *A Defence of Freemasonry* (1765), contains "A Song by Brother S. Smart, A.M. Tune, 'Ye frolicksome Sparks of the Game.' "

XI *Arrest and Rescue*

That Smart had need of all the friends he could muster soon became evident, for shortly after the publication of *Translation of the Psalms,* his printer, Dryden Leach, had him arrested for a debt of eighty-six pounds. Evidently a number of the subscribers, who had paid the original required half-price of the volume, had failed to pick up volumes on publication. Thus Smart cannot be held totally responsible for his getting in debt. The humiliation and despair felt by Smart over the situation can be seen in a letter from Granville Sharp, the philanthropist, dated January 3, 1766, to John Sharp, then Archdeacon of Northumberland. The archdeacon, who had evidently subscribed for ten copies of the *Psalms,* had failed to pick them up. Granville Sharp quoted from a letter he had received from Smart, who wrote inquiring about the disposal of the ten books. Smart said that he "must have finished an unfortunate life in jail had it not been for the good nature of a Friend, who could not bear to see his tears."[14] Granville Sharp, who had himself picked up the ten copies and asked the archdeacon for instruction concerning them, concluded his letter by expressing a wish that some sort of employment might be found for Smart, who seemed very capable of earning a good living.

Because of the generous aid of Smart's "Friend," no public record of Smart's arrest exists. Confirmation of Smart's rescue from prison—through the good offices of a friend—occurs, however, in another of Smart's letters, dated January, 1766, from "Storey's Gate Coffee House, St. James's Park." In this letter—written to a Welshman, Paul Panton—Smart again relates the story of his plight and rescue; he concludes with an appeal for aid toward another volume of *Miscellaneous Poems.* Although the *Miscellaneous Poems* were advertised in the verse translation of Horace, they were never published.

But the year 1767 saw a brief revival of Smart's fortunes. His friend Mason had organized a subscription to aid Smart. Another friend, Stonhewer, who had become private secretary to the Prime Minister of 1766, managed to get Smart on the list of Expectants for a Poor Knight of Windsor: a note in the *Domestic Entry Book* for April 26, 1766, indicates that the king intended to give him the next place as Poor Pensioner at St. George's, Windsor. Although the poet was never to enjoy the benefit of the post, which carried an annuity, he no doubt was gratified at the recognition given him. An even more important event occurred in the following year: the publication in 1767 of the verse translation of Horace mentioned in Hawkesworth's letter.

Addressed to Sir Francis Blake Delaval, Smart's constant and aristocratic patron, the translation of Horace appeared in four handsome volumes. With his verse translation, Smart included a prose interpretation "for the help of students" and occasional notes. In the preface the poet speaks with some feeling of the necessity of his having to do such a work—as he had previously noted in his preface to the prose translation. He notes, however, that he had set about his work with a consciousness of a talent attested to by the great scholars of his day, including Mr. Pope. He concludes with a mention of his ancestry and suggests that he might have done better if he had been working on a production more suitable to his background and talents. While the verse translation is better than Smart has intimated—it is a testimony to his talent and industry—it was a commercial failure.

XII   *Last Days Before Imprisonment*

In December, 1767, John Newbery died. His will designated one-third of his estate to Anna-Maria, with the proviso that she alone could sign any receipt and that no part of her heritage could at any time be under the control or subject to the debts of her husband. About this time Anna-Maria sent her two daughters to be educated in a convent in France; she also befriended French émigrés (one of whom, Chevalier Jean de la Brousse Le Noir, married Elizabeth in 1795) and established a Roman Catholic chapel in Reading. Smart's response to the will and to his daughters being sent to a foreign convent is not known, but it may have been bitter enough to estrange him further from his immediate family and its religion.

Smart continued to write, and in 1768 he brought forth another oratorio, *Abimelech;* but it was not reprinted and seemed of mediocre quality. Probably it was simply another effort to keep up with the poet's devouring debts; for, despite his fifty-pound allowance from the treasury and other helps, Smart continued to have money troubles. A more praiseworthy work in the same year by the poet was *The Parables of Our Lord and Saviour Jesus Christ,* inscribed "Done into familiar verse, with occasional applications for the use and improvement of younger minds." The volume, which consisted of all the parables of Christ, along with many other scenes from the Bible, contained over three thousand lines. These parables, dedicated to Bonnel George Thorton, the three-year-old son of the wit with whom Smart had been friendly, received some favorable comment. But the volume was not very popular and was never reprinted. Smart's hope that such a work would be adopted by parents and teachers was doomed to disappointment.

Because most of his publications since 1762 had been commercial failures, they seemed to injure rather than help Smart with his publishers. The booksellers and printers became increasingly distrustful since they had to bear most of the loss. Smart's prospects disintegrated, and he finally had to depend, aside from his fifty pounds from the treasury, entirely on his friend Mason's subscription scheme for support. This dependence proved a humiliating one for Smart, who was often obliged to write the subscribers to remind them of their promises. Such a reminder was a letter the poet wrote to Paul Panton on January 4, 1768, reminding him that this was "the Anniversary of Mason's kind plan," and asking him for his subscription of two guineas. Although Panton made an effort toward having the subscription paid the following year without a begging letter from Smart, the poet was again obliged to ask for the subscription in January, 1769.

Smart's second letter to Panton reveals, in addition to the reminder, evidence of his continued hopes that he would still inherit under the will of Francis Smart. The poet's grandfather had died the previous year, leaving the poet nothing in his will. Christopher, who was heir-at-law, contested the will; and, in his letter to Panton, he denounced the misfortune which made it necessary for him to beg a couple of guineas when he was direct heir to a property worth six hundred pounds a year. But a few months later, on July 29, 1769, Smart was obliged to sign an indenture showing that his position as heir-at-law gave him no claim to Francis's estate. Smart received a nominal five shillings for signing this quittance, but he remained convinced that he should have been heir to the ancestral lands and a house at Staindrop Moor.

His final, forced renunciation of his claim to the ancestral estate proved to be an almost fatal blow to Smart's own self-esteem and also to his financial condition. He became more and more destitute, and even those friends who had been so loyal—at least many of them—seemed to desert him. But a few remained loyal to the end; one of these was Dr. Charles Burney, whom Smart continued to visit. In her diary Fanny Burney describes such a visit Smart made her father: "Mr. Smart the poet was here yesterday....This ingenious writer is the most unfortunate of men—he has been twice confined in a mad-house—and but last year sent a most affecting epistle to papa, to entreat him to lend him half-a-guinea!—How great a pity so clever, so ingenious a man should be reduced to such shocking circumstances. He is extremely grave, and still has great wildness in his manner, looks, and voice." It is impossible to see Smart, comments Fanny, without feeling sorry for him.

On October, 1769, Fanny records another visit in her diary: "Poor Mr. Smart presented me this morning with a rose....'It was given me,' said he, 'by a fair lady—though not so fair as you!' "[15] Fanny archly remarks that the *Critical* reviewers—who had suggested that Smart's declining powers made him a likely candidate for a third confinement in Bedlam—would be even more confirmed in their judgment should they hear such a compliment. The girl's comment is valuable in that it shows an opinion concerning Smart's mental condition that seems to have been common to the day; a man named Shaw wrote that he believed Smart insane and that he intended to withdraw from the poet as a consequence.

But in the general withdrawal of Smart's friends, a notable exception was Thomas Carnan, his brother-in-law, who came forward to help him at this crucial period. Perhaps at the prompting of Anna-Maria, and perhaps because of his own pity for the poet's unfortunate condition, Carnan seemed to have made some efforts in Smart's behalf. A letter from Smart to Carnan, dated April 16, 1769, demonstrates Smart's thankfulness that some action might be taken so that he should not go to prison. A meeting between the two men is suggested to that end.

XIII *Imprisonment and Last Period Before Death*

Carnan's efforts, however, were not enough to save the poet from prison. In April, 1770, he was arrested and taken to the King's Bench Prison, at the bottom of the old Borough Road, Southwark, on a complaint lodged by a James Bright. On April 26 Smart was formally committed because he could not provide bail. Other complaints by Bright followed, and probably there were many others which could have been brought forward. The paying of Bright's bill would simply have meant that the other creditors would have been forthcoming.

Although Carnan could not save Smart from prison, he did secure for the poet the "Rules" of the prison—the "Rules" referred to a small area round the prison where debtors who could pay were allowed to walk. Without Carnan's act, Smart would have been confined without respite to an unspeakably squalid cell. Other friends, headed by Dr. Burney, made up a small subscription to supplement the miserly prison allowance. Smart expressed his gratitude in a note to Dr. Burney, remarking, "I bless God for your good nature, which please take for a receipt." Another note from the poet to Dr. Burney shows Smart's deep sympathy and response to the sufferings of others: in it Smart pleads for a fellow prisoner who needed help, one whom the poet has already helped, he says, "according to my willing poverty."[16]

From the prison he saw his last work, *Hymns for the Amusement of Children,* published on December 27, 1770, through the help of Carnan. This little volume, priced six pence, did not carry his name—probably to avoid bringing his creditors down upon it. This work for children must have brought some happiness to Smart in his last dark days; he had abandoned his messiah obsession and spoken of his belief in God's faithfulness and mercy. Both the creating and the publication of the work helped to reaffirm the poet's faith.

In the last few months of his life, Smart, broken by illness and starvation, had fallen into almost complete despair. His note to a friend, the Reverend Jackson, speaks of a recovery from a recent illness, "and having nothing to eat, I beg you to send me two or three shillings, which (God willing) I will return, with many thanks, in two or three days."[17] He died on May 20, 1771, after a short illness described by Hunter as "a disorder of the liver." Seccombe's account in the *Dictionary of National Biography* states that Smart was buried in St. Paul's Churchyard, but it seems impossible to confirm this statement. There is no record of his name or burial in the cathedral. As Devlin remarks, "This seems a little sad, for St. Paul's was the mansion of his dreams in which he saw himself 'the Reviver of ADORATION amongst ENGLISH-MEN.' "[18]

While the circumstances of Smart's last days were grim and dark, he died a poet and a man of God. Edith Sitwell has said of Smart: "There was no room in the heaven of this madman's mind for cruelty or injustice, or for anything but love. That Heaven was undimmed by the cruelties and darkness of prison, unbroken by starvation, warm in the midst of that deathly cold. This madman of genius, this poet of genius, for all the barriers of his madness, continued to walk in the cool of the evening with his God."[19]

CHAPTER 3

Smart's Early Work

The early work of writers is frequently of negligible interest and value—either biographically or literarily in regard to its influence on the writer's later and more notable products—but Christopher Smart's writing was from the beginning almost wholly concerned with events in his life, his personal interests, his religious concerns, and his literary goals. The interests of his early writings are repeated almost into his final work; they show his continuing loyalty to, and affection for, the scenes of his early life and for those who were dear to him. Above all, some of his early lines reflect what was to be his life work: the praise of God through poetry.

I *Poems of Childhood*

A little jingle composed, according to Margaret, the poet's sister, when Smart was four years old, demonstrates his early interest in ladies. According to the account of the incident, young Christopher was very fond of a young lady about three times his age who had been affectionate toward him. A gentleman old enough to be the girl's father teased Christopher by pretending to be a rival and threatening to marry her. "You are too old," retorted the little boy. The gentleman then suggested he would send his son. Christopher answered this threat in a love poem mentioning his rival and asking the girl to take his part. The little poem concludes with the lines requesting, "Madame, if you please to pity/ O poor Kitty, O poor Kitty."[1]

Christopher Smart doubtless wrote other small poems, but a more ambitious effort was his "To Ethelinda," an ode composed when he was thirteen. As before related, this ode resulted in an attempted elopement, but the attempt was thwarted with no ill feelings. To some critics, "To Ethelinda, on Her Doing My Verses the Honour of Wearing Them in Her Bosom" seems to have a highly amorous air somewhat precocious for a thirteen-year-old boy. Containing four stanzas, the poem begins, "Happy verses! that were prest/ In fair Ethelinda's breast!" Each of the four stanzas contains six lines of rhyming couplets and the second stanza begins, "Oft thro' my eyes my soul has flown,/ And wanton'd on that ivory throne." This stanza concludes: "Tell me, is the omen true,/ Shall the body follow too?" His last lines advise her to throw his verses "from that downy bed,/ And take the poet in their stead."

Cyril Falls suggests that "there is about the piece a warmth of passion uncomfortable, whether artificial or not."[2] Critics who think along these lines tend to believe that Smart suffered damaging effects from his disappointment over this youthful love affair. They suggest that his subsequent loss—Anne Vane married Charles Hope-Weir in 1746—may have started him on his career of dissipation. Smart's passion for Anne Vane may have been, on the other hand, simply the kind of transient love affair which leaves no scars. Devlin believes that Smart at thirteen had already decided to be a poet; the poet found himself "in love" and expressed his "passion" through his ode. This critic observes that "The honeyed impudences of Elizabethans and Cavaliers—or perhaps directly his own Horace and Catullus—were the only models he knew. The result was an exercise in bad taste, but the style was reasonably taut and economic."[3] In any event, "To Ethelinda" was the first of several poetical references to Anne Vane.

II *Cambridge and Early Period in London*

Smart, who continued his experimentation during his Cambridge days and the early period of his residence in London, explored a wide range of subjects and concerns. The large amount of miscellaneous verse identified with this period shows that Smart tried his hand at almost every form and type of poetry popular in his day: light verse, the ode, epitaph, epigram, ballad, fable, and occasional poem. The diversity of his early talent and effort can be seen in his *Poems on Several Occasions,* published in 1752. In this work Smart tried to include most of the verse he had written up to that time, except the Seatonian prize poems. He reprinted the Tripos poems, which were in Latin, as well as odes, epigrams, and fables which had appeared under the wide assortment of strange pseudonyms he affected in such periodicals as the *London Magazine*, the *Gentleman's Magazine*, *The Student, The Midwife*, and *The Reading Mercury*.

In addition to his Tripos poems, Smart also included other translations of Pope's *Essay on Criticism* and *Ode for Music on St. Cecilia's Day*, and a Latin version of Milton's *L'Allegro*. Translations of these and other works such as Samuel Butler's *Hudibras* in Latin demonstrated Smart's skill in translation. In his original work in Latin he displays the wit and ingenuity for which he was famous, but little of this body of verse is of interest today.

Several old favorites, also written at Cambridge and included in the *Poems*, were "On Taking a Bachelor's Degree," "On an Eagle Confined in a College Court," and "The Pretty Barkeeper of the Mitre." Smart also printed his youthful "To Ethelinda," which appeared on the second page of the volume. It is interesting to look at some of Smart's other early work—not only verses from the 1752 *Poems*, but also similar early pieces collected in Hunter's 1791 edition of Smart's poetry—to see the variety of styles and traditions in which he wrote.[4]

III   *The Pastoral*

One of the traditions of early interest to Smart was the pastoral, inspired perhaps by the century's admiration for Milton's *L'Allegro* and *Il Penseroso*, and for James Thomson's *Seasons*. Smart's two companion pieces, *On Good-Nature* and *Against Ill-Nature*, in octosyllabic and decasyllabic rhyming couplets, are rhetorical attempts to follow the manner of *L'Allegro* and *Il Penseroso;* the pieces contain such Miltonic passages as the opening lines: "Hail cherub of the highest heav'n/ Of look divine, and temper e'n," and "Slander's vip'rous tongue." Other Miltonic echoes can be heard in Smart's Pindaric *Ode to the King*, written in 1748. The ode tells, "Of Camus oft the solitary strand/ Poetically pensive still I haunt." The song continues, ". . . now no more Bellona's brazen car/ Affright's Urania in her blissful seat."

Also in the pastoral tradition are three companion pieces: "A Morning Piece, Or an hymn for the haymakers"; "A Noon-Piece, Or, The Mowers at Dinner"; and "A Night Piece, Or, Modern Philosophy." All three poems are light and happy in tone, with a kind of jauntiness. In the morning, "Brisk Chanticleer his matins had begun." The human figures in "A Morning" include the villager Colin, reclining on his rake as he sings. Of the passage, "Strong Labour got up—With his pipe in his mouth,/ He stoutly strode over the dale," Goldsmith commented, "There is not a man now living who could write such a line."[5]

"A Noon-Piece" contains, among conventional pastoral figures, a less typical picture of faithful Tray guarding the dumpling and the whey, as well as Collin Clout and Yorkshire Will swilling from a leathern flasket. The poet also pays tribute to his oft-mentioned love, Miss Harriot Pratt. He tells her that, if he could decoy her to these meads, "New grade to each fair object thoud'st impart,/ And heighten ev'ry scene to perfect joy." The last of the trio, "A Night-Piece," faintly foreshadows Smart's later exotic quality in the lines, "Night with all her negro train,/. . .In an hearse she rode reclin'd,/ Drawn by screech-owls slow and blind."

A short masque, *The Judgment of Midas,* also in the pastoral tradition, is a rather pleasing portrayal of the contest between the "Celestial candidates," Apollo and Pan. The songs of each contestant and his followers, in blank verse and rhyming couplets, are conventional and fairly ordinary. Upon Midas's choosing Pan, Apollo has the judge crowned with a pair of "ass's ears" and proclaims: "Such rural honors all the gods decree,/ To those who sing like Pan, and judge like thee."

IV *The Hop-Garden*

Another version of the pastoral, the long blank-verse poem, partly didactic and partly pastoral, is Smart's *The Hop-Garden.* This work, a georgic in two books, was written in the manner of the English georgic, where directions in verse were given for performing some agricultural task, the whole framed by descriptive and topographical poetry. A famous example of the form is *Cyder,* by John Phillips. While the versified directions in the georgic were of doubtful value to farmers of the time, they enjoyed some popularity. In the Augustan intellectual climate, poems modeled on the lesser work of Virgil could hardly fail to appeal. John Phillip's georgic in eighteenth-century Miltonics seemed to lend dignity and nobility to the subject; and his imitators, including Smart, encumbered their themes with the same heavy Miltonic diction and overly elaborate Latin vocabulary.

Concerning *The Hop-Garden,* Hunter wrote that not much commendation could justly be given—either to the poetry or to the instructions. "The Author," writes Hunter, "seems to have addressed himself to the task without previous information on the art which he treats."[6] But, since hops were native to Smart's native country, observed Hunter, they had to be "adorned by the Muse." Most critics feel that Smart's rules for growing hops are for the most part accurate but that they are marred by Miltonic versification. *The Hop-Garden* has, however, its rewarding passages, especially those expressing Smart's awareness and poetic response to the beauties of natural life and of the countryside. As Grigson has noted, a reader who looks at *The Hop-Garden* with a retrospective sympathy will find in it "a number of those first sensory impacts, those metallic illuminations, which were to obsess Smart later in the creative excess of his vision."[7]

At the feet of the hop grower, says Smart in his poem, flows the "silver Medway." Farther on, "midst th' hoary leaves/ Swell the vermillion cherry; and on yon trees/ Suspend the pippin's palatable gold." The beauty and grace of fish always attracted Smart, and he describes, "silver bleak and prickly pearch,/ That swiftly thro' their floating forests glide." From the sturdy woodman's ax, "Down tumble the big trees, and rushing roll/ O'er the crushed crackling brake." At night, "bright Chanticleer explodes the night/ With flutt'ring wings, and hymns the new-born day." An early baroque image occurs when Dorinda, building the Christmas pudding, finds amond the dried foreign fruit a "negro's nail." An early reference to Orpheus occurs when a shepherd whistles and "The green whisper, and the big boughs bend"; for it was ". . .thus the Thracian, whose all-quick'ning lyre/ The floods inspir'd, and taught the rocks to feel." Orpheus is later to be identified with the great psalmist of *A Song to David*.

Throughout *The Hop-Garden* are legends of Saxon times. Especially interesting is the story of Roxena, daughter of Hengist, who mixed a magic potion fatal to enamored Vortigen. Hengist then usurped Vortigen's seat in Kent and reigned for a long time. But now, says the poet, the palace walls are razed—"Perchance on them/ Grows the green hop, and o'er his crumbled bust/ In spiral twines ascends the scancile pole." In the story of Roxena there is a theme often repeated in Smart's work: the interaction of art and nature, of the wild and the composed. In Roxena's duplicity, the poet notes that even her artificial tears looked natural, ". . .for ev'n art to her,/ Was natural, and contrarieties/ Seemed in Roxena congruous and allied."

The very hop land itself, notes the poet, is an alliance of art and nature. Not "towering pines, nor lofty elms,/ Nor the meadows green,/

Nor orchats, nor the russet mantled nymphs" attract his eyes as does the yonder hop land: "Joint-work of Art and Nature." In his celebration of Shipbourne, his birthplace, the poet speaks of Fairlawn, ". . .where at once at variance and agree,/ Nature and art hold dalliance."

In Smart's nature material Robert E. Brittain sees "an essential happiness" as its most important characteristic. The critic observes, "In the period in which he [Smart] wrote, such nature material as appears is almost always handled in a mood of gentle melancholy or in a way which reveals a basic distrust. The great exception to this statement is of course Thomson, but even his work reveals these qualities at times."[8] Brittain notes that, while a few traces of these qualities appear in Smart's early work, the poet's mature work is free of them. Smart, comments Brittain, never sees nature as an alien and hostile power. On the contrary, in one of his hymns the poet writes, "Gentle nature seems to love us/ In each fair and finished scene." This same spirit of joy in nature prevails in *The Hop-Garden.*

V *Epigrams, Epitaphs, and Fables*

Besides his experiments in the pastoral, Smart also wrote a number of epigrams, epitaphs, and fables. In an early epigram, "On a Malignant Dull Poet," written while he was at Cambridge, Smart alludes to the spit venom of the snake making a wound which can be cured by the snake's own fat. Thus it is, says the poet, with ". . .the blockhead who ventures to write;/ His dulness an antidote proves to his spite." Another four-line epigram, "On the Merit of Brevity," comments on Smart's efforts at waggery. If the reader thinks, the poet observes, that his works have too much levity, he should at least approve his brevity; for ". . .our Bards at this Time are confoundly tedious." Another humorous epigram, "An Epigram of Sir Thomas More, imitated," mentions the fair Dorinda who outwits her lover by placing her "Lily hand" behind her back and daring him to kiss there—if her long nose interferes with his kissing her lips. In a more serious mood is the epitaph, "On the Death of Master Newbery," a dignified and sympathetic tribute to a young boy.

A more homely verse form than the epigram, and a great favorite with Smart, was the fable. Smart modeled his fables after those of John Gay, who had popularized the fable form in the previous quarter-century. In the poet's own era, the fables of William Wilkie, John Langhorne's *Fables of Flora,* and the later ones of Cowper demonstrated the popularity of the genre; and Smart's pieces came to have some vogue. He published the first of his own fables in *The Midwife* of 1750, and in 1765 a poetical translation of the fables of Gudius. Of the nineteen fables published in Hunter's 1791 collection of Smart's poems, only these few appeared in the 1752 *Poems:* "The Bag-Wig and the Tobacco-Pipe," "Care and Generosity," "Fashion and Night," "Where's the Poker?" and "The Teapot and the Scrubbing Brush." Other fables, "The Brocaded Gowne and Linen Rag," "The Duellists," "The Snake, the Goose, and the Nightingale," appeared in the 1754 volume of the *Gentlemen's Magazine;* in the 1755 volume were "Mrs. Abigail and the Dumb Waiter" and "The Country Squire and the Mandrake." A small quarto edition of poems by Smart published in 1763 contained *Reason and Imagination.* Others no doubt appeared first in various periodicals of the period.

All of the fables are in octosyllabic couplets and in colloquial diction, with nonsensical rhymes. They are mainly concerned with the affairs of everyday life. Since most of the fables are similar in theme and style, they are considered as representing some of the poet's early interests.

One of Smart's concerns was cruelty to animals. While still at Cambridge, he protested such treatment in his poem, "On an Eagle Confin'd in a College Court"; he scorned not only those who would confine such an imperious spirit to a "service cell," but those who could walk by and view such captivity with indifference. In his fable, "A Story of a Cock and a Bull," also protesting cruelty to animals, Smart opens with a humorous comment on contemporary British complacence about their land and its inhabitants. Woe to him, laughs Smart, who dares to deny that "One Englishman's worth ten of France." But, although we British excell in "arts and arms,/ In learning's lore and beauty's charm," says the poet, "Would we'd a little more humanity." In the story a bull, grown old and feeble in faithful service, is sent to the fair to be baited. There is pathos in the dignity of the bull who returned and "with stern silence inly mourned." The cock, like the bull, had faithfully served—he had been "hour-glass, guard, and clock"—and had also returned wounded and in pain. Hearing the bull's moans, the cock urges him to rise and scorn man's ingratitude, for perhaps there will come a change:

> Methinks I hear from out the sky,
> All will be better by and by;
> When bloody, base, degenerate man,
> Who deviates from his Maker's plan;
> Who Nature and her works abuses,
> And thus his fellow creatures uses,
> Shall greatly, and yet justly want,
> The mercy he refus'd to grant.

Thus Smart indicts not only man's cruelty toward animals but his exploitation of them—the works of nature—for greed.

In "The Citizen and the Red Lion of Brentford," the poet depicts a citizen who is berated by a lion painted on a tavern sign because he has allowed himself to be imposed upon by spongers. Remember the tale of poor Acteon, says the lion, who was "by the dogs he fed devoured." The lion advises the "Cit" (Smart has already identified himself with the Citizen) to go back to bed: "You're better and you're cheaper there,/ Where are no hangers on to fear." The Citizen thanks the lion and promises him a new coat for his good advice. Also concerned with the dire results of overly lavish hospitality is "Care and Generosity." Smart recommends generosity with care—the golden mean.

Smart's continuing battle with critics is reflected in several of his fables. "The Wholesale Critic and the Hop-Merchant" condemns the contemporary critics who "judge by prejudice and parts" instead of trying to comprehend the whole of a work. Some critics, he says, seem to judge by the quantity and weight of the material, others by proportion, form, and "gilding." The Critic, Tom Catchup, ridicules the merchant for judging and buying a large quantity of hops on the basis of a random handful. The merchant retorts that the critic has judged ten volumes by a page and that the critic erroneously judges himself to be one of universal knowledge: "Art, trade, profession, calling, science;/ You mete out all things by one rule,/ And are an universal fool."

A happier jabbing at the critics is "The Pig." In it, a group of wits and wags are unable to distinguish a real squeal of a pig from the imitation by a prankster. Indeed, they especially deride the real squeal with cries of "Pshaw! Nonsense!" Honest Hodge produces the real pig and advises: "Behold, and learn from this poor creature,/ How much you critics know of Nature." Still carping on the critics, Smart entitles another fable "The Snake, the Goose, and Nightingale," with a pointed subtitle: "Humbly addressed to the hissers and cat-callers attending both Houses." The poet declares he welcomes "the critic's rod" when it is "ruled by truth and nature's way." But, when critics are "inflamed by spite alone," they are as one and have no right to class themselves as individuals. Thus, the debate between the snake and the goose as to who plagiarized the other's hissing at the nightingale's song cannot be resolved. The nightingale reminds these critics that they are, in their hissing, like no other animals; they should, therefore, be kind as brother to brother.

The snobbishness of tawdry elegance is set against the independent spirit of homely virtue and usefulness in "The Tea Pot and the Scrubbing Brush." Taunted by the Tea Pot, the Scrubbing Brush declares that she does not shine because she is making others do so and that the Tea Pot is "fair without and foul within." Many girls today, comments the Scrubbing Brush, would be better off if they got their "bloom and glee" by wielding a scrubbing brush instead of peddling scandalous gossip. Times won't mend, the poet decides, "Til some Philosopher can find,/ A scrubbing-brush to scrub the Mind."

The same contrast between tawdry splendor and wholesome virtue and the use of homely things is underlined in a more ambitious fable, "The Brocaded Gowne and Linen Rag." There is a slight nationalistic suggestion in this poem: the brocaded gown is French, from Paris, a hand-me-down from a lady to her maid; beside the brocaded gown in the closet hangs a linen rag, somewhat soiled. With a *French* shrug, the brocaded gown rustles indignantly and speaks in an injured tone of her close proximity with a filthy rag. But the linen rag says that the brocaded gown ("At once so ancient and so easy,/ At once so gorgeous and so greasy") cannot anticipate the rag's great destiny. The rag will be washed by the Medway and be used to make fine paper on which will be immortalized the verse of noteworthy contemporary writers. Some of these "sons of genius" whom Smart extols include Arthur Murray, Akenside, Collins, "our great Augustan Gray," and Mason ("Learning's first pride, and Nature's too"). The linen rag ends by contrasting her glorious fate with that of the brocaded gown who, she predicts, will end in a dunghill or a sty. Smart has used this fable as a vehicle for compliments to other writers; but he is also making moral comments about the disparity between appearance and intrinsic worth, as symbolized by the gaudy French gown and the soiled linen rag.

In "The English Bull Dog, Dutch Mastiff, and Quail," Smart makes a plea for national tolerance. He asks, "Are we not all of race divine,/

Alike of an immortal line?" It is false to judge "the heart or head,/ By air we breathe, or earth we tread." One should throw prejudice to the wind, and "be patriots of mankind." The English Bull Dog and the Dutch mastiff praise their own nations and abuse other lands. The quail tells them they are both wrong, that "Mankind is not so void of grace,/ But good I've found in every place." In this fable Smart again protests, incidentally, the cruel treatment of animals: the quail is captive, even in England, the boasted land of freedom. Smart also mentions the woes of Ireland and Hartington's aid to the country, which seems to fix the date of composition as April, 1755.

Reason and Imagination, a fable addressed to Mr. Kenrick, tells the story of exotic lady Imagination who, being weary, longs for a mate. To Reason, studying in a little cottage, Imagination sends a message: he is too grave and hard-working; she can take him "To those bright plains, where crowd in swarms/ The spirits of fantastic forms." She can be at once Reason's tutoress and wife. But Reason answers, "I'm lost, if e'er I change my state./ But whensoe'er your raptures rise,/ I'll try to come with my supplies." Smart concludes with a tribute to Kenrick, "happy in the view/ Of *Reason,* and of *Fancy* too." He takes the liberty of advising Kenrick not to be decoyed from the Bible—"The truth to full perfection brought,/ Beyond the sage's deepest thought;/ Beyond the poet's highest flight."

VI *The Ballads*

Smart wrote a number of ballads, many of them poems to "the fair," with personal references, written during his Cambridge days. "The Pretty Bar-Keeper of the Mitre," written in 1741 while the poet was in college, describes how all were entranced by the charms of the barkeeper, whose bosom was not hidden by a handkerchief, and who had "heaving breasts with moles o'erspread,/ Markt, little hemispheres, with stars." In both "Sweet William" and "To Jenny Gray," two other early ballads, Smart depicts conventional catalogues of poetic flowers adorning chaplets for the hair of Sweet William and Jenny.

Still concerned with a lady, but ending on a more cynical note, is a brief cantata, "The Widow's Resolution." The recitative and air alternate in a description of Sylvia, a widow whom swains pursue in vain. But she is finally won, and Smart comments on the enchantment of "beauty weeping at her weeds." Since a lover cannot return from death, "All the pomp and farce of mourning/ Are but signals for a new."

One of the poet's several tributes to Miss Harriot Pratt is "Lovely Harriote," which the poet calls "A crambo ballad." Here he declares that "Virtue, Beauty, Truth, and Love,/ Are other Names for Harriote." He ends the ballad by swearing by Hymen and the powers haunting Love, "So sweet a Nymph to marry ought." His "To Miss H——, with some Music" is subtitled "Written by a poet outrageously in love." But Smart renounces Harriot and all his past loves in "The Lass with the Golden Locks," dedicated to Anna-Maria Carnan, who was to become his wife. He sings, "To live and to love, to converse and be free,/ Is living, my charmer, and loving with thee."

VII   *Satire and Verse Epistles*

There are many suggestions of the influence of Horace on Smart, and one of the earliest was Smart's *The Horation Canons of Friendship,* published in June, 1750. *The Canons,* appearing under the pseudonym of Ebenezer Pentweazle, is an imitation of the third satire of the first book of Horace. The poet dedicated his *Canons* to the Shakespeare editor, John Warburton. Beyond the poet's use of the heroic couplet to convey Horatian sentiments, the work is undistinguished. In a humorous satire, addressed to "my good friend, the Trunk-Maker of the Corner of St. Paul's Churchyard," Smart suggests that his works will probably be used to line trunks.

Smart was especially adept at the verse-epistle, a very popular form of the era; and his epistles, usually in octosyllabic couplets, are of interest biographically in showing his affection, humor, and warmth of feeling toward his friends. A typical example is "To the Rev. Mr. Powell." (On the nonperformance of a promise he made to the author of a hare). The poet begins, "Friend, with regard to this same hare,/ Am I to hope, or to despair?" The "Epistle to Dr. Nares" invites the doctor to dinner and advises his prospective guest of some of the dishes he may look forward to: a goose, "With apple-sauce and Durham mustard,/ And cooling-pie o'er laid with custard." In his postscript the poet adds, "I have, (don't think it a chimaera)/ Some good sound Port and right Madeira." The same gay spirit of hospitality invests "An Invitation to Mrs. Tyler" (A clergyman's lady, to dine upon a couple of duck on the anniversary of the author's wedding day). The happiness of Smart's marriage had not yet been dimmed by trouble, and he writes, "Tomorrow is the gaudy day,/ That day, when to my longing arms,/ Nancy resigned her golden charms."

Later and especially valuable from a biographical point of view is "An Epistle to John Sherratt, Esq.," which appeared in June or July, 1763, the year of Smart's release from confinement. John Sherratt seems to be the one who actually obtained freedom for the poet. Smart confirms in this epistle the fact that he had been more or less in confinement for seven years; he mentions his appreciation of Sherratt's goodness which has—above the undoubted blessing of his visits "in hold"—been able to "set the pris'ner free." To Sherratt the poet pays this tribute: " 'Tis you that have in my behalf,/ Produced the robe and killed the calf;/ Have hail'd the *restoration* day." The poet plays one more note on his lyre—to gratitude—and affirms, "One gift of love for thee remains;/ One gift above the common cast." Sherratt's "distin-guished deed" is one whose spirit is "open and avow'd/ Arrayed itself against the crowd." Such a deed stands for ever on record—"IF TRUTH AND LIFE BE GOD AND LORD."

VIII   *The Seatonian Prize Poems*

An important part of Smart's early works were his Seatonian prize poems, written between 1750 and 1755. The donor of the prize, Mr. Thomas Seaton, bequeathed his estate in 1738 to the University of Cambridge. The income was to maintain a yearly prize open to all graduates for the best poem in English on a subject assigned by the vice-chancellor, the master of Clare-Hall, and the Greek professor, who were also judges of the contest. For the first year the subject was to be "one or other of the perfections or attributes of the Supreme Being, and so the succeeding years, till the subject is exhausted; and afterwards the subject shall be either Death, Judgment, Heaven, Hell, Purity of Heart, &c. or whatever else may be judged. . . most conducive to the honour of the Supreme Being and recommendation of virtue."[9] Smart won the Seatonian prize in 1750, the first year it was offered, and every one of the other four years he entered for it. His first poetical essay, *On the Eternity of the Supreme Being,* was published in April, 1750; for it he received thirty pounds in prize money, a very welcome addition to his income.

The judges awarded the Seatonian prize to Smart in 1751 for *On the*

Immensity of the Supreme Being; in 1752, for *On the Omniscience of the Supreme Being* in 1753, for *On the Power of the Supreme Being.* In 1954, the Seatonian prize was awarded to George Bally for *The Justice of the Supreme Being;* Smart did not submit an entry that year—perhaps illness prevented his doing so. In 1755, he waited so long before submitting his *On the Goodness of the Supreme Being* (1756) that he barely had time to write it and send it as quickly as possible to Cambridge so as to be within the required time for submitting entries. In 1756, the poet became insane; and his connection with the college was broken by the time he was again able to write acceptable verse.

Smart's Seatonian poems were all written in blank verse, with many Miltonic overtones of compound epithets, inversion, and suspension. Written in his new life as a journalist in London, the Seatonian poems offered Smart a chance to maintain a tie with the university world he had left and to write dignified verse in contrast to the trivia he was turning out for the London periodicals. But the greatest value of the prize poems lay in their being a kind of training ground for the poet's great endeavor, *A Song to David.* As Grigson has pointed out, Smart's vision was given its trial run in the Seatonian poems: "Smart's ultimate grandiloquence crystallizes in a conjunction of the natural and the grandly visioned, the curiously observed and the grandly imagined, a baroque vision, as if a soaring, crowded, sparkling, coloured, active, three dimensional interior, shall I say, of an eighteenth-century German baroque church of the Brothers Adam or Dominikus Zimmerman, full of flowers, fruits, figures, emblems, immediacies and infinities, and scraps of reflective surface, had been condensed and simplified in Protestant terms."[10] For even the ineptness of the Seatonian blank verse does not obscure entirely the vivid language and the tone of fervor with which Smart attacked his difficult, abstract subjects. Many rudimentary concepts and images later brought to their full glory in *A Song to David* find their first expression in the Seatonian prize poems.

In the progression of the Seatonian poems, the idea of Smart as a psalmist in the succession of David develops and becomes explicit. His first poem begins with a salute to God: "Hail, wond'rous Being." And he asks, "May then the youthful, uninspired Bard/ Presume to hymn th' Eternal?" But in the second poem, *On the Immensity of the Supreme Being,* he allies himself more closely with the line of poets praising God: "Once more I dare to rouse the sounding string,/ *The poet of my God*—Awake my glory,/ Awake my lute and harp." The words of David open *On the Power of the Supreme Being* (1754); "'TREMBLE, thou Earth,' th' anointed poet said,/ 'At God's bright presence, tremble, all ye mountains,/ And all ye hillocks on the surface bound.'"

In the last of the poems, *On the Goodness of the Supreme Being* (1756), Smart again alludes to David—with even more point and emphasis. The poet identifies David of the Hebrews with Orpheus of the pagans: "ORPHEUS, for so the Gentiles call'd thy name,/ Israel's sweet psalmist, who alone could wake/ Th' inanimate to motion." Smart asks David to infuse something of his spirit "in this breast/. . . And lift me from myself; each thought impure/ Banish; each low idea rise, refine,/ Enlarge and sanctify."

Smart began in these Seatonian poems the rich catalogue of wonderful creations of the universe that later illuminates *A Song to David*. God, indeed, is "Immense Creator! whose all-powerful hand/ Fram'd universal Being, and whose Eye/ Saw like thyself [David], that all things form'd were good." Grigson has brilliantly commented concerning the Seatonian poems:

In these poems, these annual liftings of Smart from the Grub Street of London, he not only combined detail of earth and the choir of heaven, he combined his experience of a limited and a wider nature, observation with reading, his own eye with the eye of travellers, naturalists, and scientists,—the known to him with the imagined by him. The Supreme Being, eternal, immense, omniscient, powerful and good. His seraphim and His cherubim, are conjunct in the poems with—for example— astronomical phenomena, sun, moon, comets, stars, planets, Saturn and his ring. Meteorological or optical concerns, refraction, colours, rainbow, thunder, hurricane, join heaven to earth; on earth the 'central magnet', and ores, fossils, crystals, gems sparkling in the deep mines of Gani, Roalconda, Peru, Ceylon, the Pyrenees, diamond, jasper, garnet, moss-agate presenting its curious pictures, and ruby . . . — all these encounter corals, pearls and amber observed in sea-depths; and these hard brilliants are in turn associated with other activities, other strange or brilliant items of the created earth: with earthquakes and eruptions and molten fire; with cataracts, caves, lakes, mountains; with beasts: lion, elephant, Leviathan, African camels (carrying ingots of gold); with insects: ant, glow-worm, bee; with birds: woodland warblers, woodlark, redbreast, linnet, ring-dove, jay, nightingale, peacock, raven; with flowers: tulip, auricula, peach blossom, lilies, roses, hawthorn, pansies, deadly nightshade, dock, hemlock; with fruit: pomegranate, pineapple, cherry, plum, and these again with the spices and gums of Arabia; all in a geographical range outwards to the Antarctic.[11]

The rather conventional rhetoric and temper of the Seatonian poems are the result perhaps of the poet's awareness of the eighteenth-century distrust of "enthusiasm" and his feeling that he should curb any intellectual or theological extravagance—for the winning of the prize was important to him.

IX *Hymn to the Supreme Being*

The Seatonian poems were written during the Grub Street period of Smart's life, and with them may be considered another devotional poem, *Hymn to the Supreme Being, on Recovery from a dangerous Fit of Illness* (1756). This poem is written in six-line stanzas with the rhyme scheme *ababcc*. The first five lines in each stanza are in iambic pentameter, and the last line is an Alexandrine. This poem is of interest not only for its biographical content, but also for its indication of the poet's developing artistic powers. Its form is lyrical, anticipating Smart's rejection of other poetic forms. The poet prefixed his poem with a testimonial addressed to Dr. Robert James concerning the benefit the poet derived from Dr. James's "Fever Powder."

Hymn to the Supreme Being opens with a biblical reference to the sickness of King Hezekiah, who recovered from a dangerous illness through a reprieve from God. The king had pleaded the blamelessness of his life when asking to be spared. For his own return to well-being, Smart feels that he cannot plead such justification. He sends back his memory over his past, but "Home, like the raven to the ark, she flies,/ Croaking bad tidings to my trembling ears." Through heavenly mercy the poet is saved; his health returns, and "exil'd reason takes her seat again—/ Brisk beats the heart, the mind's at large once more,/ To love, to praise, to wonder and adore." Smart speaks in affectionate terms of his wife and children whose tears have not been shed in vain.

In the following stanzas, Smart praises the qualities of God already celebrated in his Seatonian poems: the eternal nature of God, His immensity, omniscience, and goodness. God's justice could never have been withstood, the poet asserts, except by the mercy given us by Christ's acts: "He rais'd the lame, the lepers he made whole,/ He fix'd the palsied nerves of weak decay,/ He drove out Satan from the tortur'd soul"; above all, Christ regained his "lost fallen flock" with his taintless blood. In addition, Christ's pity has gained for the poet a second birth.

In lines illumined with some of the poetic genius of *A Song to David,* Smart dedicates himself solely to God:

> Ye strengthen'd feet, forth to his altar move;
>> Quicken, ye new-strung nerves, th' enraptured lyre;
> Ye heav'n-directed eyes, o'erflow with love;
>> Glow, glow, my soul, with pure seraphic fire;
> Deeds, thoughts, and words no more his mandates break,
> But to his endless glory work, conceive, and speak.

While extolling, in the closing stanzas, the glorious creations of God—the rose, the eagle, the Leviathan, the lion, and gold—Smart reminds the world that none can compare to man. So man's purpose should be to serve and obey. The last stanza of the hymn is Smart's promise to justify his miraculous delivery: "That I may act what thou has giv'n to know,/ That I may live for THEE and THEE alone."

Devlin has remarked that in this hymn Smart has gone back a century and a half to the great beginnings of English religious verse. Of Smart's poetic resolution this critic comments: "There is a great glory in the way he rises from his sick-bed a completely new man, mind and heart wholly intent upon his Maker and Redeemer; there is glory in the way he sets about immediately, like a busy workman, to pound and shape the golden language of Spenser till it glows and vibrates with quite a new power of God-directed thought and feeling. It is a laborious work at first; but here at last is the man who will write *A Song to David.*"[12]

But Smart was not able immediately to pursue his intention. For in the same year—1756—of the publication of the *Hymn to the Supreme Being,* Smart began his seven years of confinement. In the madhouse he wrote a manuscript but recently discovered, *Jubilate Agno.*

CHAPTER 4

Jubilate Agno

I *Discovery of the Manuscript*

Although Christopher Smart celebrated his recovery from a dangerous illness with his *Hymn to the Supreme Being,* published in 1756, he was, in fact, on the brink of madness. He was under some kind of restraint during that year, and he remained principally under confinement until 1763—a period of seven years. A literary record of his experience, *Jubilate Agno,* written by Smart during this period, thus becomes one of the most curious and valuable portions of his writing. This document supplies not only names, dates, and other information about a hitherto unknown period, but also gives added information about Smart's poetic preparation for his great *A Song to David.*

The discovery of the autograph manuscript, by a remarkable coincidence, came about because of the madness of another poet, William Cowper. Two friends of Cowper, William Hayley and the Reverend Thomas Carwardine, made extensive investigations into Cowper's affliction. In the course of their enterprise, *Jubilate Agno,* a product of another mad poet, Smart, came to their attention; and it must have been of special interest to them because it remained in Carwardine's hands. Eventually, it came to be preserved in the library of his great-grandson, Colonel W. G. Carwardine Probert, where it was noticed by William Force Stead. Stead spent many hours of research in compiling explanatory notes and obtained permission to publish the manuscript in 1939. He called his edition *Rejoice in the Lamb, A Song of Bedlam*—a title invented by him and not by Smart. The portion found consists of thirty-two pages written in a kind of free verse. The original manuscript is now preserved in the Harvard Library.

II *Structure and Content*

Stead found only a series of rather large fragments of the original *Jubilate Agno,* perhaps less than half of the poem as Smart wrote it. Because Stead attempted to arrange these fragments chronologically, he missed the intended structure of the work. A later editor, W. H. Bond, perceived the original structure as an attempt to adapt the antiphonal or responsive character of Hebrew poetry to English verse. He arranged the parts, whenever possible, so that they could be read in conjunction, making the whole work much less chaotic than before.[1]

There are two obvious divisions in the portion found: the *Let* and the *For* sections. Every poetic line in the *Let* section, with two exceptions, begins with the word *Let;* every line in the *For* section, with one exception, begins with the word *For.* No verses beginning *For* appear in the *Let* section, and vice-versa. Smart marked his pages with catchwords: the catchword for the *Let* pages is *Let;* for the *For* pages, *For.* Thus it appears that the poet wished the two sections to remain physically distinct.

Although the *Let* and *For* sections of *Jubilate Agno* are physically distinct, they are closely related in content. The frequent occurrence of dates in the text helps to show that, on occasion, the two sections were written concurrently, with a notable agreement between the *Let* and *For* sections. The poet's original intention seems to have been for a line-for-line correspondence between the two sections, but without the missing portions it is impossible to determine how closely Smart adhered to this plan.

Before looking at the fragments in detail, it may be useful to consider a source of Smart's interest in the techniques of Hebrew poetry and its influence upon his plan in writing *Jubilate.* The poet seems to have derived much of his interest in Hebraic verse from Bishop Robert Lowth's *De Sacra Poesi Hebraeorum,* first published in 1753. In his book Lowth examined the rules governing the poetry of the Bible; he particularly emphasized the responsive or antiphonal character of Hebrew poetry.

Smart may have found the responsive principle of Hebrew verse especially appropriate for a contemplated plan dear to him: the reform of the Anglican liturgy. *Jubilate Agno* seems to have been intended as a responsive reading, closely parallel to portions of the Order for Morning Prayer and the Psalter. That Smart may have envisioned himself as the second reader or responder is suggested by the physically distinct nature of the *Let* and *For* verses. For very few of the *Let* verses, until one comes to Section D, contain any personal reference; nearly all the references relating to Smart himself occur in the *For* verses. But during the period of composition his plan and purpose changed. What began as a genuine outpouring of poetic prayer in praise of God, in responsive verse, came at last to be a mere recording of time—perhaps with a line written each day—with notes about his concerns and personal problems.

As previously noted, Bond devised a somewhat different classification of the found portions of *Jubilate Agno* than had Stead, the first editor. Bond classified the portions as Fragments A, B_1, B_2, C and D; and he divided each fragment into *Let* and *For* verses. Bond's arrangement is used in this discussion.

III   *Fragment A*

Fragment A, probably composed in the early part of 1759, begins with a call to all humanity to join with the animals of the land, the fish of the sea, the flowers, and the precious materials of the earth in a hymn of praise to their maker, God:

> Rejoice in God, O ye Tongues; give the glory to the
>   Lord and the Lamb.
> Nations and Languages, and every Creature, in which
>   is the breath of Life.
> Let man and beast appear before him, and magnify his
>   name together.
> Let Noah and his company approach the throne of Grace,
>   and do homage to the Ark of their Salvation.
> .   .   .   .
> Let Ishmael dedicate a Tyger, and give praise for the
>   liberty, in which the Lord has let him at large.
> Let Balaam appear with an Ass, and bless the Lord his
>   people and his creatures for a reward eternal. (1-11)

Stead has pointed out the coupling of man and creature which begins in this fragment and continues through the first part of the piece. As the roll of biblical flora and fauna is limited, the poet soon ran out of appropriate pairs and was forced to include nonbiblical animals in his verses—the tiger, for instance. Many of the animals in these lines from *Jubilate Agno* later appear in *A Song to David.* The *Let* verses in Fragment A are the most skillfully written of any in the poem; they show that Smart at this time was capable of ordered thinking. Unfortunately, as the *For* verses for this section are missing, it is impossible to determine the poet's entire plan for this portion. No doubt the *For* verses of Fragment A contained personal allusions—similar to *For* verses available in other fragments—which would make clearer the writer's whole conception.

IV   *Fragment B₁*

In Fragment B_1 the complete interplay between *Let* and *For* verses may be examined. Again, as in Fragment A, the poet has coupled a proper name with that of an animal, and to an extent the same impersonality can be seen. In the *For* section, however, there are more personal allusions which reveal a great deal concerning Smart's situation and his attitude toward his personal problems together with the people concerned. One of Smart's major concerns, for example, was his family; and these lines reveal his bitterness and resentment. He notes, "For I meditate the peace of Europe amongst family bickerings and domestic jars"(7). Later on he comments, "For I am come home again, but there is nobody to kill the calf or pay the musick"(15).

A reference to Smart's forced renunciation of his birthright, always a point of controversy, occurs with a *Let* passage which shows the importance of having the corresponding *Let* and *For* verses together for a complete understanding of the text. In line 46 he writes, "For I this day made over my inheritance to my mother in consideration of her infirmities." This *For* line and several following seem to imply that Smart gave up his inheritance with good will. But, as Bond points out, the associated *Let* verses reveal Smart's true attitude toward the situation. The corresponding *Let* verses are concerned with animals such as the kite, the wittall—a bird whose nest is violated by the cuckoo, symbolizing the man whose wife is unfaithful—the locust, and the gull, of whom Smart says, "who is happy in not being good for food." The association of these animals and the theme of cuckoldry with the reference to his inheritance shows Smart's real attitude toward the incident—one of bitterness and resentment.

There also occur in Fragment B_1 some references to the conditions of the poet's confinement. He comments, "For they work on me with their harping-irons, which is a barbarous instrument, because I am more unguarded than others"(124). Later he remarks, "For I bless God that I am not in a dungeon, but am allowed the light of the sun"(147). That the poet equates himself with Christ as a victim of his enemies can be seen in the line, "For I am under the same accusation with my Saviour—for they said, he is beside himself"(151).

Critic Devlin believes that Smart at this time seems to have taken upon himself the triple vow of chastity, poverty, and obedience—the early Church's interpretation of Christ's counsels of perfection. From Fragment B_1 Devlin cites the following lines to support this suggestion concerning the poet's poverty, "For tis no more a merit to provide for oneself, but to quit all for the sake of the Lord"(81); of chastity, or the desirability of chastity, "For beauty is better to look upon than to meddle with and tis good for a man not to know a woman"(104); and, concerning obedience, "For I am ready to die for his sake—who lay down his life for all mankind"(98). This threefold structure of chastity, poverty, and obedience is indicated later in the rather ambiguous passage, "For the coffin and the cradle and the purse are all against a man"(276). The coffin, explains the poet, is "for the dead and death comes by disobedience." The cradle symbolizes man's weakness; the purse, money, which the poet calls "dead matter with the stamp of human vanity."[2] In a following line the poet notes bitterly, "For the purse is for me because I have neither money or human friends"(283).

But, although Smart may have lost some of his faith in man, he still believes in the certain goodness and power of God; thus he intends to continue to use his voice for praise and prayer: "For a man speaks HIMSELF from the crown of his head to the sole of his feet"(228), and "For I bless God in the strength of my loins and for the voice which he hath made sonorous"(80).

V   *Fragment B_2*

The meditations on scientific and theological themes which are interspersed in the verses of Fragment B_1 are continued in Fragment B_2, which has no impersonal *Let* verses but consists of *For* verses only in the next two double folios. The verses contain some rather surprising sentiments. For example, he denounces the theater: "For all STAGE-Playing is Hypocrisy and the Devil is the master of their revels"(345). The poet's admiration for the comedy in college and for *Mother*

Midnight's Oratory seems to have changed; there is further evidence of this reversal of attitude toward the theater in succeeding fragments.

Other verses show Smart's continuing affection for the things of the earth—notably flowers. He was allowed to make a garden during his confinement, as the following anecdote makes clear. After returning to London in 1760, after an absence of nine years, Burney asked concerning "poor Smart," and whether or not he was likely to recover. Johnson said that the poet was at least growing fat on his illness. When Burney suggested that perhaps this was the result of lack of exercise, Johnson replied, "No, Sir; he has partly as much as he used to have, for he digs in his garden."[3]

To Smart, flowers are "great blessings" and "the poetry of Christ." He ascribes to them esthetic, religious, scientific, mystic, and medicinal qualities. The flower passage contains some lovely lines; especially striking—if rather ambiguous—is the following: "For the Lord made a Nosegay in the medow with his disciples & preached upon the lily"(494). Smart had introduced the "nosegay" motif in Fragment B_1 : "For the Lord Jesus made him a nosegay . . ."(105). And the last line of the flower passage repeats, in B_2, the same note: "For the Poorman's nosegay is an introduction to a Prince"(510)—a personal suggestion concerning the poet's poverty and his offering of flowers as a gift to God.

VI *The Cat Jeoffrey*

Fragment B_2 closes with the famous passage concerning the poet's cat Jeoffrey—a mere accidental ending, the result of the loss of part of the manuscript. Smart had already mentioned Jeoffrey in Fragment B_1 : "For I am possessed of a cat, surpassing in beauty, from whom I take occasion to bless Almighty God"(68). In B_2 he pays a long tribute to Jeoffrey; the lines open, "For I will consider my Cat Jeoffrey./ For he is the servant of the Living God and duly and daily serving him./ For at the first glance of the glory of God in the East he worships in his way"(697-99).

Following is an intricate series of movements tracing the course of Jeoffrey's day, and this note about the day's end: "For when his day's work is done his business more properly begins./ For he keeps the Lord's watch against the adversary"(719-20). Later the poet calls his cat "a mixture of gravity and waggery," and the same mixture of humor and seriousness seems to infuse this delightful description of Jeoffrey.

VII *Fragment C*

A decline in poetic achievement mars Fragment C. A gradual disintegration occurs in Smart's original plan of close correspondence between *Let* and *For* verses in the 162 parts constituting this portion, for these two sets of verses are almost wholly independent in content. Place names and personal names are chosen without discrimination and are coupled with plant names which appear to have been chosen at random. Occasionally a personal allusion holds some interest: "God be praised for this eleventh of April O.S. in which I enter into the Fortieth Year of my age. Blessed. Blessed. Blessed"(222).

Smart repeats previous themes in these lines. Orpheus is again associated with David; public prayer is still one of the poet's dearest hopes: "For I prophecy that the praise of God will be in every man's mouth in the Publick streets"(62-63). His comments on flowers, however, are poor echoes of previous lines: "For the art of Agriculture is improving./ For this is evident in flowers"(157-58). Bond has suggested that the deterioration in the verses may have been the result of renewed mental disturbance, aggravated by the poet's chafing under his involuntary confinement. Smart does, however, experiment with the meaning of letters in this fragment, a device he was later to use in the pillars passage of the *Song*.

VIII *Fragment D*

In Fragment D, consisting of two hundred and thirty-seven lines of *Let* verses, the deterioration is complete. The poet has abandoned biblical names and has apparently chosen both the personal names and the names of natural objects at random. At times—indeed, very early—occur such unrelated ideas as the following: "Let Ross, house of Ross, rejoice with the Great Flabber Dabber Flat Clapping Fish with hands. Vide Anson's Voyage & Psalm 98th ix"(11). His references offer some help in interpreting his meaning, but not much.

Smart also refers to efforts being taken to secure his release from confinement: "Let Metcalf, house of Metcalf rejoice with Holcus Wall-Barley—God give grace to my adversaries to ask council of

Abel"(159). Stead interprets "my adversaries" to mean those who had committed him to the asylum, and "to ask council of Abel" to suggest that they be given grace to make an end to the poet's confinement. Among the poet's last lines is a reference to John Sherratt, who led in gaining Smart's release: "Gentle God be gracious to John Sherratt"(235).

As Stead has suggested, the value of *Jubilate Agno* is twofold: it gives insight into the sources of *A Song to David,* and it enables those interested in Smart to learn much about the poet that is unobtainable elsewhere.[4] The places which had been dear to him, the friends who continued to hold him in high regard, his affection for flowers and for small animals are only a few of his many themes. Smart's faith in God never wavered—there is no questioning of God concerning the poet's predicament. Throughout this period he continued to keep his vision of his mission on earth. In writing the chaotic, irregularly strange and beautiful *Jubilate Agno,* Smart prepared himself in part for *A Song to David.* Without this period of meditation in the asylum and without his written expression of his days there, his greatest poem might never have been written.

Poet George Barker finds a link to the modern spirit in *Jubilate Agno:* "When, in I think 1936 I (and the rest of the world) came upon the *Jubilate Agno* it was like drawing the curtain on a fine spring morning. I think it almost the only long poem in English that is stark naked. This poem OUGHT to be the New Testament of the Beat Poets."[5]

CHAPTER 5

A Song to David

In April, 1763, a few months after Smart's release from confinement, his *A Song to David* appeared. The poet's masterpiece was published by M. Fletcher, of the Oxford Theatre in St. Paul's Churchyard, to sell at the price of one shilling; every copy was signed by the author. At the close of the poem the writer included proposals for printing by subscription *A Translation of the Psalms of David* and *A Set of Hymns for the Fasts and Festivals of the Church of England.* The *Translation,* in addition to *Jubilate Agno,* probably served as a training ground for *A Song,* for there are references to the writing of the verses in Smart's madhouse manuscript.[1]

A Song to David met with a lukewarm reception from its contemporary readers. William Mason, an old friend from Smart's Cambridge days, wrote Thomas Gray, "I have seen his *Song to David* & from thence conclude him as mad as ever."[2] A typical eighteenth-century reaction. Even the sparse praise was reserved. The *Critical Review* remarked, "great rapture and devotion is discernible in this ecstatic *Song* . . . it is a fine piece of ruins."[3]

The commonly felt opinion of the century regarding *A Song* in relation to Smart's other writings was expressed by Christopher Hunter, the poet's nephew, in his preface to the 1791 edition of Smart's poems: "Besides the poems contained in this edition our Author wrote a poem called *A Song to David* and a New Version of the Psalms. . . . These, with two small pamphlets of Poems, were written after his confinement, and bear melancholy proofs of the recent estrangement of his mind."[4] Instead, remarked Hunter, he had included poems he thought would be acceptable to his readers. Thus not only *A Song* but all of Smart's postconfinement writing was excluded as being undesirable.

I   A Song *in Browning's* Parleyings

Robert Browning, a century later, perceived the true value of *A Song to David;* he considered it, however, the poet's only notable achievement. In his *Parleyings with Certain People of Importance in Their Day* (1887), Browning celebrated Christopher Smart; and he conceived an elaborate metaphor relating to Smart's poetry in general and to *A Song to David* in particular. Browning pictures himself as an explorer of a huge house, going from room to room, where abounded "decent taste" and "adequate culture," but where "All showed the Golden Mean without a hint/ Of brave extravagance that breaks the rule." Suddenly he enters the chapel—*A Song to David*—and is overwhelmed by its glory:

> . . . from floor to roof one evidence
> Of how far earth may rival heaven. No niche
> Where glory was not prisoned to enrich
> Man's gaze with gold and gems, no space but glowed
> With colour, gleamed with carving-hues which owed
> Their outburst to a brush the painter fed
> With rainbow substance"[5]

When Browning paid this tribute to *A Song to David,* he regarded the work as the product of a mad poet, an attitude fostered by a legend that Smart had written it on the walls of his madhouse cell. But not only is it hard to believe that a poem of five hundred and sixteen lines could have been scratched on wainscoting, but the manuscript *Jubilate Agno* shows that Smart was not deprived of pen and paper while in confinement. He may have begun the *Song* while he was confined; but, if it had been completed by the time he was released in January, 1763, he would have published it at once—he needed the money. The April publishing of the work suggests that he completed it in the few months following his release, or that he wrote it in its entirety from January to April.

II   *Sources of* A Song to David

A Song to David is a complicated poem. But some of the passages seem difficult and obscure because Smart drew from his recollections of a wide variety of reading, and many of his sources are not commonly known. Smart's taking from his vast storehouse of remembered material is remarkably evident in earlier writing, particularly in his madhouse manuscript, as William Force Stead has ably shown in *Rejoice in the Lamb*. Brittain also comments concerning Smart's wide range of reference in *Jubilate Agno:* "Hundreds of people whom he had met at one time or another, an even greater number of characters he had read about in the Bible and elsewhere, and a prodigious multitude of animals, birds, fish, reptiles, plants, and even stones whose English, Latin or Greek names he had come across years before in the works of a variety of 'natural historians'–all these, together with a strange assortment of 'facts' gathered from scientists, pseudo-scientists, and mystics, are brought together in a strange medley."[6]

This drawing from many sources is characteristic to a lesser degree of *A Song to David*. One of his most important sources was, of course, the Bible, especially the accounts of David's life in Samuel, books one and two. Other biblical sources include the Genesis account of the Creation, drawings from the Psalms and other sacred books, both canonical and apocryphal. There were also many details from a book called *An Historical Account of the Life and Reign of David, King of Israel*, written by Patrick Delany, a friend of Swift, and published in London, 1740-42. Smart had read Delany's book as early as 1755 because he refers to it in a footnote on the opening lines of *On the Goodness of the Supreme Being*.

Evidence of some of Smart's earlier work appears in the *Song*. From his translation of Horace, Smart adopted Horatio's attitude concerning the use of obsolete words, archaisms, and peculiar application of words. Sophia Blaydes remarks, "It is little wonder that early readers attributed the strange blend of Hebraism, Horation language and eighteenth-century music to madness. Yet the sources are not in themselves unusual; it is in the blending and mixing, which is astonishing in its complexity and technique, that is definitive of Smart and his genius."[7]

A last source is the Masonic observance. Smart was a Mason, as he demonstrated in *Jubilate Agno* and the *Song*, which contain Masonic symbols obscure to the uninitiated. Thus Smart was able to evoke more than one meaning from a particular image or section, lending special richness to the *Song*. An example can be seen in the passage of the *Song* concerning the pillars of knowledge. The immediate source of the reference to the pillars is a text of Proverbs IX supposed to have been written by David. Other references occur in Near Eastern mystery religions, in cabalistic and neo-Platonic works which interested Smart, and in legends of freemasonry. A Masonic lodge is reputed to stand on the three pillars of wisdom, strength, and beauty.[8]

III   *Subject*

With this wide background of reading and research, Smart began to write *A Song to David*. In an advertisement of the first edition printed in *Poems on Several Occasions* (1763), the poet called his masterpiece "a poem composed in a Spirit of Affection and thankfulness to the great author of the Book of Gratitude, which is the Psalms of David the King."[9] It was natural and fitting that the poet should choose the life and works of David as the subject of his poem and as the central figure through which to extend his concept of religion. The figure of David had long been an inspiration to the poet, and no doubt the work Smart did on the Psalms increased his admiration for the Hebrew king. Seeing the Psalms as a "Book of Gratitude," Smart believed that David had expressed the true purpose of man: to praise and adore God. Indeed, Smart believed that all creation *did* express deep gratitude for God's goodness and mercy.

David was an authority on praise of God. Using David as an instrument of praise reinforced Smart's own theology. Although Smart was a member of the Anglican Church and abided by its doctrines, he developed a personal, although not heretical, religious view. He believed in trichotomy, the idea that man is the image of the Holy Trinity, an opinion that was not new to Smart; for he declares in *Hymn XVI,*

> Man, soul, and angel join
> To strike up strains divine,
> O blessed and ador'd,
> Thine aid from Heav'n afford;
>   HOLY, HOLY, HOLY, THREE,
>   Which in One, as One agree.

Again in the *Song* he says, "Man's made of mercy, soul, and sense." Blaydes suggests, "The idea then created a chain of being which links all creation: man, soul, angel and God. The *Song* emphasizes the chain of being; it becomes one of Smart's minor themes, as well as a reinforcement of David, who is the best man, akin to the angels, and so on."[10]

The selection of David as the subject of the *Song* may have supported the belief that the poem was the product of a madman. For, while David had his admirers in the eighteenth century, he was the topic of much adverse criticism because of his uprising against Saul, his causing Jonathan to defect, and his association with Bathsheba. The battle that ensued between David's admirers and critics has been noted by Arthur Sherbo in *Christopher Smart: Scholar of the University*. But Smart saw David as God's foremost adorer.

IV   *Themes and Structure*

Smart's themes, suggests Brittain, have nothing especially strange about them; the real difficulty and complexity of the poem lie in its intricate technique of expression. But here also, the critic says, lies its real power: "in the sheer intellectual and artistic ingenuity with which the main themes are stated, elaborated, varied, and intensified by the manipulation of a number of minor themes around them."[11] One aspect of the poet's technique is his adapatation of what Brittain calls "the climactic building up of a series of concepts which embody certain similarities."[12] Tracing a series through the varied kingdoms of life became Smart's favorite use of the method. He used this structure in the early Seatonian poems, the *Hymn to the Supreme Being,* the *Psalms,* and the *Hymns;* he also used it in *A Song to David.*

Several other critics have also commented on the structure of the poem. Sir Edmund Gosse, in his essay on *A Song in Leaves and Fruit* (1927), has pointed out the orchestral effects of the work. Another critic, Signor Frederico Olivero, in his essay *"Il 'Canto a Davide' di Christopher Smart,"* translated by Brittain, calls the poem a kind of temple in its symmetry and precision of structure: the invocation becomes the series of steps leading into the temple; the facade consists of the figure of David in twelve statues with various attitudes; and so on to the final exaltation of David as a forerunner of Christ, which marks the height.

Olivero also points out the extreme accuracy and the connected arrangement of the details of the *Song.* The images are not, he comments, independent and unrelated to each other. As stanza follows stanza, there is a symmetrical relationship of the images or central thoughts in one stanza to those in the stanza following and succeeding stanzas, so that the whole becomes like an intricately woven garland. By using comparison and contrast, the poet develops an orderly procession of thought. Olivero gives as an example of this technique the poet's image of light in the depiction of the sun, stars, and comets (Stanza LXXXIV, 1-3) correlating with the image of the aurora borealis in Stanza LXXXV, 1. Especially notable, thinks Olivero, are the elegant groupings of exotic trees, flowers, and fruits which correspond to each other from strophe to strophe in a subtle and almost imperceptible gradation.[13]

One of the most valuable examinations of the architecture of the *Song* is Raymond D. Havens's essay. "The Structure of Smart's *Song to David.*" Havens remarks that Smart constructed the *Song* with unusual attention to parallelism, formal design and pattern, a pattern of mystic numbers. The entire poem, he suggests, is made up of stanzas in groups of threes or sevens—the mystic numbers—or their multiples.[14] The analysis of the structure of the poem by Professor Havens and the working out of the details by Brittain are followed for the most part in the following examination of the lines.

V *Form and Contents*

A Song to David is a lyric composed of eighty-six stanzas of six lines each with the consistent rhyme pattern *aabccb*. This stanzaic form, romance-six, was popular during the age. The *aa* and *cc* lines are in iambic tetrameter, and the *b* lines in iambic trimeter. While occasional trochees, dactyls, and anapests for emphasis are used throughout the poem, a relative smoothness and consistency occur. A sustained beat and a harmony of theme and structure reflect the eighteenth-century correlation between music and literature. Blaydes has compared the *Song* to some of the great religious music of the age—especially to Handel's—in its harmony, religious spirit, and attention to form.[15]

Perhaps Smart wrote his "Contents" at the suggestion of the printer. He seems to have written it hastily and to have ignored obvious divisions in the poem. Smart may have been too close to the poem to analyze it objectively, or he may have been too impatient to get his poem in print to give his "Contents" special attention. Nevertheless, the "Contents" shows the poem to be far from the emotional outpouring of a madman—as some of his contemporaries thought it to be. He worked with thought and restraint, and embodied his major concepts in a general design:

Contents. Invocation, ver. 1,2,3.—The excellence and lustre of David's character in twelve points of view, ver. 4; proved from the history of his life, to ver. 17.—He consecrates his genius for consolation and edification.—The subjects he made choice of—the Supreme Being—angels; men of renown; the works of nature in all directions, either particularly or collectively considered, to ver. 27.—He obtains power over infernal spirits, and the malignity of his enemies; wins the heart of Michal, to ver. 30.—Shews that the pillars of knowledge are the monuments of God's work in the first week, to ver. 38.—An exercise upon the decalogue, from ver. 40-49.—The transcendent virtue of praise and adoration, ver. 50 and 51.—An exercise upon the seasons, and the right use of them, ver. 52 to 64.—An exercise upon the senses and how to subdue them, from ver. 65 to 71.—An amplification in five degrees, which is wrought up to this conclusion, "That the best poet who ever lived was thought worthy of the highest honor which possibly can be conceived, *as the Saviour of the world was ascribed to his house, and called his son in the body."*

VI   *Invocation: Stanzas I-III*

The poem begins with what Smart calls an "Invocation" of three stanzas. This section introduces the two main motifs of the poem: first, the hailing of David as the great king, the servant of God, and the supreme poet and singer in praise of the Almighty; and, second, the themes of gratitude to God and praise for God's mercies and benefits. For the two—gratitude and praise—are closely bound together. A suggestion of the intended scope of the poem appears in Stanza II: "To bless each valley, grove and coast,/ And charm the cherubs to the post/ Of gratitude in throngs."

In the last stanza of the trio Smart calls David God's "minister of praise." The poet asks David to listen and appear from his high eminence to receive the wreath (the poem) Smart has woven for him—his tribute to the great Hebrew king.

I

O Thou, that sit'st upon a throne,
With harp of high majestic tone,
    To praise the King of Kings;

And voice of heaven-ascending swell,
Which, while its deeper notes excell,
    Clear, as a clarion, rings.

II

To bless each valley, grove, and coast,
And charm the cherubs to the post
    Of gratitude in throngs;
To *keep* the days on Zion's Mount,
And send the year to his account,
    With dances and with songs.

III

O Servant of God's holiest charge,
The minister of praise at large,
    Which thou may'st now receive;
From thy blest mansion hail and hear,
From topmost eminence appear
    To this the wreath I weave.

VII   *Stanzas IV-XVII*

The next section (Stanzas IV-XVI) begins in Stanza IV with a
declaration concerning—as Smart states in his "Contents"—"The excellence and lustre of David's character in twelve points of view." These
twelve qualities of David are ennumerated: "Great, valiant, pious, good,
and clean,/ Sublime, contemplative, serene,/ Strong, constant, pleasant,
wise." Smart attached great importance to the twelve virtues, and
Brittain has indicated the occurrence of the motif in earlier works.[16]
From *Jubilate Agno* are the lines:

For there be twelve cardinal virtues—three to the
    East—Greatness, Valour, Piety.
For there be three to the West—Goodness, Purity &
    Sublimity.
For there be three to the North—Meditation, Happiness,
    Strength.
For there be three to the South—Constancy, Pleasantry,
    and Wisdom. (B$_2$, 355-58)

In another passage from *Jubilate Agno,* Smart associates the twelve virtues, not with the points of the compass, but with the tribes of Israel and with some contemporary acquaintances:

> For there be twelve cardinal virtues the gifts of the
>   twelve sons of Jacob.
> For Rueben is great. God be gracious to Lord Falmouth.
> For Simeon is Valiant. God be praised to the Duke of
>   London.
> For Judah is Good. God be gracious to Lord Granville.
> For Dan is clean—neat, apt, active, compact. God be
>   gracious to Draper.
> For Naphtali is Sublime—God be gracious to
>   Chesterfield.
> For God is contemplative—God be gracious to Lord
>   Northampton.
> For Asthur is Happy—God be gracious to George Bowes.
> For Issacher is Strong—God be gracious to the Duke
>   of Dorsett.
> For Zebulon is Constant. God be gracious to Lord Bath.
> For Joseph is pleasant. God be gracious to Lord
>   Bolingbroke.
> For Benjamin is wise—God be gracious to Honeywood.
>   (B$_2$, 603-15)

Brittain has commented: "The evident reason for Smart's description of David's character in terms of these twelve virtues is that David may be chosen as the embodiment of all that was finest in the Israelites—the epic prototype of his people."[17]

This section is developed in an orderly way, with straightforward exposition and little counterplay of themes. The material is not difficult—most of it is derived from Samuel. Some ideas, however, seem to have been suggested to the poet by his reading of Delany. Several phrases in the section have been clarified by comparison with Delany's book, as will be noted in the examination of the stanzas.

In depicting David's twelve virtues, Smart devotes one stanza to each of the twelve virtues and exemplifies each virtue by incidents in David's life. The virtue "Valiant," for example, he illustrates in the story of Goliath. David triumphed when he took "Against the boaster from the brook,/ The weapons of the war." David is "Good" because of his desire "To pity, to forgive, to save." He demonstrated this goodness when he refused to take the life of Saul—his great enemy—when the king was at his mercy in the cave of Engedi. David's love for God and friendship with Jonathan reflect his third quality—constancy.

Stanza XVI begins, "Wise—in recovery from his fall/ Whence rose his eminence over all," a reference to David's sin in desiring Bathsheba and sending Uriah to his death. Brittain finds Smart's probable source for this idea in Delany's *Life and Reign of David:* "millions have fallen, . . . as *David* did, but who ever repented and recovered like him?" Before his sin, Delany points out, David was wise, generous, pious, and valiant. After his "hour of guilt," David led a life of meditation and "repentance before God." A passage in Delany may also account for the last two lines of Stanza XVI: "Wise are his precepts, prayer and praise,/ And counsel to his child." David, says Delany, did not neglect his son; for he left him many precepts scattered throughout the Proverbs.[18]

Concerning Stanza XVII the "Contents" says, "He consecrates his genius for consolation and edification." Devlin calls this stanza "a dark and tender connecting verse, like an archway";[19] and there seems to be, in addition, a personal identification of Smart with David:

> His muse, bright angel of his verse,
> Gives balm for all the thorns that pierce,
>   For all the pangs that rage;
> Blest light, still gaining on the gloom,
> The more than Michal of his bloom,
>   The Abishag of his age.

The "Michal" of the last two lines is David's first wife, and Abishag is the Shunammite woman who nursed David in his last illness. Smart's own muse might have been the giver of "balm for all the thorns that pierce," his "Michal" and "Abishag."

VIII   *Stanzas XVIII-XXVI*

The next section—Stanzas XVII-XXVI—Smart devotes to the subjects of David's poetry, which are, according to the "Contents," "The Supreme Being, angels, men of renown; the works of nature in all directions, either particularly or collectively considered." The themes of David's poetry concern God and all his works, visible and invisible. The first two stanzas (XVIII-XIX) of the section are concerned with the invisible: "God—the mighty source/ Of all things—the stupendous force/ On which all strength depends," and "Angels—their ministry and meed."

The next stanzas (XX-XXVI) speak of the visible works of God: "Of man—the semblance and effect/ Of God and Love—"; of "The world—the clustring spheres he made"; of "Trees, plants, and flow'rs . . ./ Gem yielding blossom, yielding fruit"; "Of fowl—e'en every beak and wind/ Which cheer the winter, hail the spring"; "Of fishes—ev'ry size and shape,/ Which nature frames of light escape,/ Devouring man to shun"; "Of beasts—the beaver plods his task;/ While the sleek tigers roll and bask"; "Of gems—their virtue and their price,/. . . The jaspar of the master's stamp,/ The topaz gleaming like a lamp/ Among the mines beneath." Each work of God praises the creator in its own way.

Brittain points out that in this section Smart begins his method of introducing minor themes into his dominant theme.[20] Among the descriptions of nature, for example, is the theme of the contrast between the natural and the cultivated—a theme found throughout the rest of the work. He sets the quail, the bird of nature, next to the "brave domestic cock." Smart further complicates the design of theme-within-theme by alternating the reference. In Stanza XXV he places two wild animals beside two tame animals but varies their response to life within the theme. The two wild animals perform the cultivated task and display natural delight in the world: the beaver plods, and the tigers roll. Similarly contrasted are the activities of the two tame animals: the rabbit makes her home, and the kids play. Smart describes, "Her cave the mining coney scoops;/ Whereo'er the mead the mountain stoops,/ The kids exult and brouse."

IX   Stanzas XXVII-XXIX

This passage is concerned with David and the effects of his song on earth and in heaven. The "Contents" says of David, "He obtains power over infernal spirits, and the malignity of his enemies; wins the heart of Michal." Stanza XXVII shows David kneeling at his harp and speaks of the power of his music: ". . . satan with his hand he quell'd,/ And in serene suspense he held/ The frantic throes of Saul." Following stanzas (XXVIII-XXIX) speak of further magic in David's playing, and of how Michal smiled, "As blush to blush she stood;/ And chose herself the queen."

X   *Stanzas XXX-XXXVIII*

According to the "Contents," Stanzas XXX-XXXVIII "Shews that the pillars of knowledge are God's works in the first week." The poet's concept of the pillars is derived from Proverbs IX, 1: "Wisdom has builded her an house; she hath hewn out seven pillars." The carvings on each pillar represent God's work on each of the seven days of creation, according to the account in Genesis. Brittain suggests that Smart was trying to show that all possible knowledge is contained in the knowledge of the works created in each of the seven days, and that the poet found this knowledge in David.[21]

But, as with other of Smart's works, the lines contain several levels of meaning consistent with the general theme. For each of the seven pillars—in the following stanzas—is introduced by a Greek letter: Alpha, Gamma, Eta, Theta, Iota, Sigma, and Omega. The letters and their significance have puzzled critics from the first appearance of the poem. An anonymous reviewer of the poem, writing in the *Monthly Review* (April, 1763), offered the following explanations of the letters: "These, we conjecture, are made choice of, as consecrated for the following reasons. *Alpha* and *Omega,* from a well-known text in the Revelation. *Iota, Era,* and *Sigma* because they are used to signify our Saviour, on altars and pulpits. *Theta,* as being the Initial of God; and *Gamma,* as denoting the number three, held sacred by some Christians."[22] Brittain suggests that, if the anonymous reviewer's theory is correct, "then it becomes clear that this subsidiary theme is the repeated names of the Deity, carrying the implied idea that all knowledge springs from and is comprised in the concept of God."[23] Smart did have some acquaintances and friends on the staff of the *Monthly Review;* he may have talked over the question of the pillars with one of them. At any event, he did not refute the theory.

Other explanations of the Greek letters include the suggestion that the letters have Masonic significance—Smart mentioned in *Jubilate Agno* that he was a Mason. Devlin, who discounts this suggestion, cites the inability of those with knowledge of Masonic ritual to offer any solution to the puzzle. From *Jubilate Agno* Devlin takes the following clue for his own explanation: "For Christ being A and Ω is all the intermediate letters without doubt./ For there is mystery in numbers"(C, 18-19). Devlin suggests that the letters should be taken as their equivalent numbers in Classical Greek. But more important, believes this critic, is that the seven stanzas describe seven aspects of Christ; he gives the last line of the introductory stanza (XXX): "From Christ enthroned to man" in support of this belief.

Thus, says Devlin, the seven pillars span from Christ enthroned to Christ, the man. Taken with the obvious meaning that the pillars stand for the days of creation, this interpretation suggests that each day represents "not only a stage in creation but an aspect of God becoming Man. This means that the incarnation of God the Son and the creation of the universe are part of the same plan."[24] Devlin analyzes each of the seven stanzas in support of his suggestion that Smart related the creation of the world with the incarnation of Christ. The first stanza, beginning, "Alpha, the cause of causes, first/ In station, fountain whence the burst/ Of light, and blaze of day," starts the evolvement. *Alpha* symbolizes the original light spoken of in the line, "Let there be light." It is also the Son coming from the Father: *"Deum de Deo, Lumen de Lumine."*

The Gamma stanza begins: "Gamma supports the glorious arch/ On which angelic legions march." Gamma, says the critic, symbolizes the creation of the upper heaven and the angels who live there; Christ is a kind of High Priest of creation. Gamma, the number three, denotes spiritual perfection found in Christ. Devlin also notes that the images in lines 1 and 2—the glorious arch and marching angels—and the image in line 5 describing the painted folds are borrowings by Smart from his own translation of three verses in Psalm 104: "who stretchest out the heavens like a curtain . . . who maketh the clouds his chariot . . . who maketh his angels spirits, his ministers a flaming fire." The image of heaven "with sapphires pav'd," comes from Exodus XXIV, 10: "And they saw the God of Israel: and there was under his feet as it were a paved work of sapphire stone; and as it were the body of heaven in his clearness."

The third stanza, Eta, refers to the creation of all growing things on the third day: "Eta with living sculpture breathes,/ With verdant carvings, flow'ry wreathes." At the base of the pillar in this stanza are carved "All instruments of labour grace,/ The trowel, spade, and loom." Eta as seven, says Devlin, is three upon four and signifies perfect growth; Christ here is the Son of God who walked with Adam in the Garden of Eden, the Christ of Nature.

The fourth stanza, the Theta one, describes the creation of the sun and moon which Smart commemorates in the beautiful lines: "And one address'd his saffron robe,/ And one, clad in a silver globe,/ Held rule with ev'ry star." Theta, suggests Devlin, stands for eight, or four upon four, symbolizing marriage—the union of bodily perfection. The critic cites lines from *Jubilate Agno* in which Smart had connected the sun and moon with marriage:

> For the Sun's at work to make me a garment & the Moon
>   is at work for my wife.(B_1 ' 111)
> . . . .
>
> For the WEDDING GARMENTS of all men are prepared in
>   the SUN against the day of acceptation.
> For the Wedding Garments of all women are prepared in
>   the MOON against the day of their purification.
>   (B_1, 192-93)
> . . . .
>
> For they are together in the spirit every night like
>   man and wife.(B_2, 319)

The image that the Theta stanza suggests, says Devlin, is that of Christ the Bridegroom, whose Bride is Israel and whose mission is turned over in the New Testament to the universal church and the whole human race.

The Iota stanza, the fifth, celebrates the day of the creation of birds and flowers. Iota, as nine, seems obscure; but Devlin identifies *nine* with maidenhood and harmony. The image of the birds and fish, Devlin contends, is the reconciliation of heights with depths; and the Iota stanza extends this reconciliation to the descent of Christ into the womb of the Virgin.

The following stanza, the Sigma one, celebrates the creation of man—among the beasts—and the birth of Christ, his appearance as true man, says Devlin:

> Sigma presents the social droves
> With him that solitary roves
>   And man of all the chief;
> Fair on whose face, and stately frame,
> Did God impress his hallow'd name
>   For ocular belief.

Devlin contends that, while all the lines except the last could refer to Adam, created in the likeness of God, the last line, "For ocular belief," could refer only to Christ, who by his appearance compelled belief in

God. There seems to be no particular significance to Sigma as a number (Sigma is eighteen), and the Sigma stanza is generally considered to be a break in the continuity of the symbols.

The sequence is restored, however, Devlin points out, with the seventh stanza in which Omega signifies twenty-four and consummation. Smart had earlier related these two in the lines from *Jubilate Agno:* "For the Four and Twenty Elders of the Revelation are Four and Twenty Eternities./ For their Four and Twenty Crowns are their respective consummations"(B_2, 361-62). In this stanza Omega is the day of rest, not only for God, but for Christ, who by his descent into hell performed the act in the last line: "clos'd th' infernal draught"—that is, says Devlin, "the down-sucking winds of the abyss." Devlin speaks of Christ—who conquered sin, destroyed death, and ascended into heaven to sit on the right hand of God; Smart traces Christ's career in his seven-pillar cycle, says the critic: "Thus *Omega* returns to *Alpha* in a circle. The sequence 'From Christ enthroned to man' goes back to Christ enthroned, but this time bearing with him human nature made immortal."[25]

The last stanza of the section salutes David and his harp. In it Smart introduces a theme he develops later in the poem: "O strength, O sweetness, lasting ripe!/ God's harp thy symbol, and thy type/ The lion and the bee!" Brittain points out that the strength and sweetness of David's "harp"—his poetry—is symbolized by the lion and the bee.

XI *Stanza XXXIX*

This brief transitional passage contains, says Brittain, "one of the most beautiful statements of the doctrine of the Holy Trinity in our poetry":[26]

> There is but One who ne'er rebell'd,
> But One by passion unimpell'd,
>   By pleasure unintic't;
> He from himself his semblance sent,
> Grand object of his own content,
>   And saw the God in CHRIST.

Brittain also finds a subtle reference to David. As the stanzas following describe a combination of God's and Christ's teachings, and as Smart hopes to present David as a moral teacher, the poet tries to answer objections to such a choice. No mortal man, David reminds his readers, is perfect, as is Christ; David is only human.[27]

XII *Stanzas XL-XLVIII*

In "Contents" Smart calls Stanzas XL-XLVIII "an exercise upon the decalogue," an enumerating of moral teachings, with David as supreme example of moral man.[28] Brittain points out that Smart tries to prove this thesis by suggesting David as the link between Moses and Christ, the descendant of Moses and the ancestor of Christ. Smart mentions Moses in this passage; later he links David to Christ in Stanza LXXXIII. The poet also mingles the Mosaic and Christian ethical codes by infusing the material of the Old Testament with the spirit and word of the New Testament. The ten commandments in Exodus, for example, are softened from the harsh Old Testament "Thou shalt not" to the more positive attitudes of Christ's Sermon on the Mount. Smart adapts or omits the ten commandments as he deems appropriate. In addition he introduces some of his own special concerns, such as, kindness to animals.

The first commandment, "Thou shalt have no other Gods before me," is given by Smart in Stanza XL as the revelation to Moses of God. The stanza begins with lines generally thought to precede the decalogue in the Protestant version: "Tell me I am, Jehovah said/ To Moses, while earth heard in dread." Immediately, "All nature, without voice or sound/ Replied, O Lord, THOU ART." This recognition of God by nature is a persistent theme throughout the poem. Smart continues the theme of the recognition of God by nature in the first lines of the following stanza (XLI), relating the theme more specifically to man: "Thou art—to give and to confirm,/ For each his talent and his term;/ All flesh thy bounties share." The poet omits the second commandment, "Thou shalt not take unto thee any graven images."

For the third commandment, "Thou shalt not take the name of the Lord in vain," Smart substitutes in the last lines of Stanza XLI the Christian commandment in Matthew V, 22: "Thou shalt not call thy brother fool." The poet has already commented in the preceding line of the stanza that all men are bound together by their debt and relationship to God. To take a brother's name in vain, then, is synonymous with taking the name of the Lord in vain.

The theme of "Be kind to animals" is central to Stanza XLII. The poet describes the nature of man: "Man's made of mercy, soul, and sense," and he suggests that man should use these qualities. The kindness-to-animals motif in this stanza is linked to the fourth commandment, "Remember the Sabbath Day to keep it holy." The poet says, "Be good to him that pulls thy plow;/ Due food and care, due rest, allow/ For her that yields thee milk." To Smart, the Sabbath should be a day of rest for animals and human beings alike. Man must feel an obligation to take care of those who serve him as God shows mercy to those who honor Him.[29]

The obedience of Christ toward God—"Not as I will, but as Thou wilt"—furnishes the poet with the example for Stanza XLIII. This stanza takes as its theme the fifth commandment: "Honour thy father and thy mother, that thy days may be long upon the land which the Lord thy God giveth thee." Blaydes considers the language of the first three lines to be reminiscent of the metaphysical school of poetry: "Rise up before the hoary head,/ And God's benign commandment dread,/ Which says thou shalt not die." Of Smart's argument in the following three lines. Blaydes remarks: "For Christ, who 'knew no guilt,' eternal life is joy, But for man, who is not perfect, the gift of eternal life carries with it the burden of control and submission to God."[30] Since man must pattern his life after Christ, he must obey his parents as Christ obeyed God.

In the next two stanzas, the poet alludes to the commandments prohibiting murder and adultery in a very delicate and indirect way. Brittain compares Smart's advice here to measures which might be suggested today by a modern psychiatrist (if he were a poet): "an exhortation to the creative use of the passions rather than a flat prohibition."[31] Smart expresses his version this way: "Use all thy passions!—love is thine./ And joy, and jealousy divine,/ Thine hope's eternal fort."

In Stanza XLVI Smart transforms the negative commandment, "Thou shalt not steal," into a request that man share what he has gained not only with the Lord but with those in need: "And make the widow's heart-strings blithe." The poet's natural sympathy for those in sorrow leads him to suggest: "Resort with those that weep." His version of the Golden Rule appears in the last lines: "As you from all and each expect,/ For all and each thy love direct,/ And render as you weep."

The last two commandments, "Thou shalt not bear false witness against thy neighbor," and "Thou shalt not covet thy neighbor's house," are also stated in positive terms by Smart. In Stanzas XLVII and XLVIII, the poet advises: "The slander and its bearer spurn,/ And propogating praise sojourn/ To make thy welcome last." Men should look forward to the future with hope, and "Look upward to the past." Bless the happy, "And for their neighbors feel."

Although confined by the traditional nature of the Ten Commandments and his verse form, Smart has managed to project his concepts in his own brilliant way. The section contains vivid imagery and language as well as some quiet, pensive moments, all enforced by his passionate, but self-contained feeling.

XIII   *Stanzas XLIX-LI*

Some difference of opinion exists among the critics about the division of the next few stanzas. Smart himself left out Stanza XLIX in his "Contents"; Grigson and Havens find it a concluding stanza to the decalogue. Brittain, who makes a grouping of Stanzas XLIX-LI, calls these three stanzas, "a traditional passage between the portions of the poem that are chiefly devoted to David and the sections devoted primarily to the great central theme of praise."[32] Stanza XLIX salutes David and admonishes him to follow "God's ways" as shown in the "genuine word"—the Ten Commandments. The last line advises: "Vain are the documents of men." For man's great duty, Smart explains in the following stanzas, is to obey and praise God.

Smart's "Contents" describes Stanzas L and LI as being concerned with a virtue: "The transcendent virtue of praise and adoration." So the lines of Stanza L direct: "Praise above all—for praise prevails;/ Heap up the measure; load the scales." There is a dual theme in this stanza: God deserves praise, and man is more likely to succeed if he praises God—"The generous soul her saviour aids."

In the next stanza (LI), there is a reference to angels: "For ADORATION all the ranks of angels yield eternal thanks,/ And David in the midst." The reference to "David" and to "angels" in this stanza, with the reference to "soul" in the preceding stanza seems to Brittain to be another example of Smart's "man-soul-angel" motif.[33] Another motif, "God's good poor," who are also a part of the admiring chorus with the angels, shows Smart's continuing concern for the unfortunate—"last and least in man's esteem." The most important function of Stanza LI, however, is to introduce the great "Adoration" stanzas, one of the most striking passages of the poem.

XIV   *Stanzas LII-LXIII*

Stanzas LII-LXIII are the first section of a two-part passage called the "Adoration" stanzas because of the repetition of the word "adoration" throughout the lines, emphasizing the theme of praise to God. Smart alters the position of the word "adoration" from the first line to the last line of each successive stanza in the first section. For example, the first line of LII is "For ADORATION seasons change." The word "ADORATION" drops to the second line in LIII: "For ADORATION tendrils climb." As each stanza contains six lines and the stanzas are twelve in number, this pattern of alteration is repeated twice.[34]

While the primary theme of the section is the praise of God, the secondary theme is the seasonal change in nature. Smart calls this section "an exercise upon the seasons and the right use of them." In orderly fashion, Smart divides the twelve stanzas into four groups of three stanzas each, the four groups corresponding to the seasons.

Besides the central themes of praise and of the progression of the seasons, the poet has introduced minor themes in this section. Brittain points out how the poet emphasizes the idea of home, with its peace and security: the bird building her nest, the mermaid and her baby, the children of Israel at peace beneath the fig tree. Again the poet has contrasted the wild and tame in his references: the cultivated "Rich almonds" are set against the bellflowers which "bow their stems," and the "playsome cubs" are linked with the beasts of the ark. Brittain also suggests that another theme—the tracing of the growth and development of man—occurs in the references to "eggs," "infant," "the coasting reader," and "labour," who "For ADORATION counts his sheaves."[35]

Part of the technical and spiritual success of this section lies in the imagery. In the spring, the "tendrils climb,/ And fruit-trees pledge their gems." The birds are busy: "And Ivis, with her gorgeous vest,/ Builds for her eggs her cunning nest." In the summer, "Increasing days their reign exalt,/ Nor in the pink and mottled vault— The opposing spirits tilt." In the fall, "For ADORATION rip'ning canes,/ And cocoa's purest milk detains/ The western pilgrim's staff." Other striking autumn images include: "rain in clasping boughs inclos'd," "vines with oranges," "apples of ten thousand tribes, "quick peculiar quince," and "wealthy crops of whit'ning rice." The last lines of the autumn passage illustrate Smart's contrast of the tame and wild: "And marshall'd in the fenced land,/ The peaches and pomegranates stand,/ Where wild carnations blow."

In the winter stanzas Smart emphasizes the beauty of the natural world and the continuation of the life process despite the snow and cold. In winter, "The crocus burnishes alive/ Upon the snow-clad earth." The "myrtles stay/ To keep the garden from dismay." Among the animals, "The pheasant shows his pompous neck;/ And ermine, jealous of a speck,/ With fear eludes offense"; the squirrel gathers nuts.

Blaydes has noted that the first section of the "Adoration" passage anticipates the second, which is concerned with the senses.[36] For there is much sensory detail of land, sea, and sky in the first section. The sense of sight is most prominently evoked and has been illuminated in the floral passages, and in the bird, animal, and oceanic descriptions depicting the seasons. Smart observes, "All scenes of painting crowd the map of nature." There is other sensory detail: the sense of touch in the lines, "to the mermaid's pap/ The scaled infant clings"; the sense of hearing in "The footed ounce and playsome cubs/ Run rustling 'mongst the flowering shrubs"; the sense of smell in the passage, " 'Mongst thyine [thyme] woods and groves of spice," and in the scent of wild carnations among the peaches and pomegranates.

XV Stanzas LXIV-LXXI

Stanza LXIV serves as a transition between the first part of the "Adoration" stanzas and the next. The reintroduction of David preserves the unity of the poem. David "kneels and chants,/ Prevails his passions to controul"–an especially appropriate reference, for the following section brings in the theme of man and his passions. There is a minor structural change. The word "Adoration" remains in the first line of the stanza and does not progress.

The second part of the "Adoration" stanzas (LXV-LXXI) comprise what the poet calls "An exercise on the senses and how to subdue them." Smart again relates the natural and the cultivated in his depiction of the five senses: touch, sight, hearing, smell, and taste. But he also introduces a human element in his depiction of adoring nature.

This fusion of natural and human is apparent in Stanza LXV: "For ADORATION, beyond match,the scholar bullfinch aims to catch/ The soft lute's iv'ry touch." The natural redbreast stands away from the "Damsel's greedy clutch."

In Stanza LXVI, Smart goes again to the skies, where "For ADORATION . . ./ The Lord's philosopher espies/ The Dog, the Ram, the Rose"/ The term "The Lord's philosopher" seems obscure, observes Brittain, until we find a footnote in Delany: "Dr. Patrick thinks, that the Greek word *Sophos,* which was originally the title of astronomers, might be derived from *Zoph,* which in Hebrew signifies a Prophet."[37] David, watching the skies, is the prophet and philosopher of the Lord. In remarking about David and the ringing planets, Smart does not forget the lowest light on earth, the glowworm, who no less adores God.

Of the "Adoration" stanzas Ainsworth has said, "All express in the highest language Smart was to reach his sublime conception of all Creation uniting in praise of the Creator."[38]

XVI   *Stanzas LXXII-LXXXVI*

The next group of stanzas, LXII-LXXXVI, Smart describes as "An amplification in five degrees, which is wrought up to this conclusion; That the best poet who ever lived was thought worthy of the highest honour which possibly can be conceived, as *the Saviour of the world was ascribed to his house, and called his son in the body.*" Each of the five "degrees" is described in a group of three stanzas, the five groups concerned being the Sweet, the Strong, the Beauteous, the Precious, and the Glorious. In the first two stanzas of each three-stanza division, Smart names the adjective and identifies it with sensory images of the natural and the cultivated. The third stanza in each trio returns again to David, who is the possessor, to the comparative degree, of the particular virtue the poet wishes to extol in that particular group of three stanzas.

Thus in Stanza LXXII, Smart catalogs and depicts the "Sweet" in sensory imagery: "Sweet is the dew that falls betimes,/. . . Sweet is the lilly's silver bell,/ And sweet the wakeful tapers smell/ That watch for early pray'r." The following stanza (LXXIII) introduces the human element: "Sweet the young nurse, with love intense,/ . . . Sweet when the lost arrive." The last stanza of the trio, LXXIV, celebrates David, whose language is linked to his "swelling chord." The theme of gratitude is introduced in the last lines of the stanza, for the poet tells David, "Sweeter, with every grace endu'd,/ The glory of thy gratitude,/ Respir'd unto the Lord."

In this section on the "Sweet," Smart employs to a high degree the poetic devices which build to a climax. The images and phrases in the beginning convey peacefulness and serenity. There is alliteration of soft consonants. In the third stanza, the consonants are harsher, and the language is more overpowering: "the swelling chord," for example. The harmony is richer and deeper.[39]

Smart continues his climactic buildup in the next trio of stanzas concerning the "Strong." The language is even more vivid and intense, the consonants harsher. The vowels have lengthened. The images conform to the intensity of the mood and purpose of the passage. The beginning lines of the first stanza (LXXV) of the trio illustrate the increased vigor and intensity of tone: "Strong is the horse upon his speed;/ Strong in pursuit the rapid glede,/ Which makes at one his game." Frequently admired for its bold and brilliant images is the following stanza:

> Strong is the lion—like a coal
> His eyeball—like a bastion's mole
>   His chest against the foes.
> Strong, the gier-eagle on his sail,
> Strong against tide, th' enormous whale
>   Emerges as he goes.

The intensity diminishes in the last stanza (LXXVII) of the group, but the lines contain a powerful theme: strong as are these forces of nature, there is someone who is stronger still.

> But stronger still, in earth and air,
> And in the sea, the man of pray'r,
>   And far beneath the tide;
> And in the seat to faith assign'd,
> Where ask is have, where seek is find,
>   Where knock is open wide.

Smart's keen, sensitive appreciation of the beautiful is demonstrated in his lovely triad (LXXVIII-LXXX) the "Beauteous," where he touches again on the things of the world, on man, and on David:

Beauteous the fleet before the gale;
Beauteous the multitudes in mail,
   Ranked arms and crested heads;
Beauteous the garden's umbrage mild,
Walk, water, meditated wild,
   And all the bloomy beds.

Beauteous the moon full on the lawn;
And beauteous, when the veil's withdrawn
   The virgin to her spouse;
Beauteous the temple, deck'd and fill'd,
When to the heav'n of heav'ns they build
   Their heart-directed vows.

Still more beautiful, the poet says in the last stanza of the trio, is David, praying with "momentous trust."

Smart checks his climactic surge with a return to a quieter mood in his stanzas concerning the "Precious." While this group checks the degree of intensity, it still retains many of the poetic devices of the fifteen stanzas on the "degrees." Many of the stanzas begin with a trochee, unlike the beginning iamb which dominated the earlier part of the work. The change of rhythm brings a new emphasis and strength. Repetition is employed to a high degree. The quality of each trio is repeated in almost every line. Alliteration is frequently employed, as in LXXXII, "Precious the penitential tear;/ And precious the sigh sincere."[40] In this trio Smart again extols David, but the poet does not forget the widow with her mite, nor "The largess from the churl," a reference from I Samuel XXV, 18. Any gift to God is precious in His sight.

The last three stanzas (LXXXIV-LXXXVI) bring the poem to an end, as Devlin remarks, "with a swelling crash, and a falling trumpet peal of 'glory.' "[41] Each line of the first two stanzas of the trio begins with the exuberant word "Glorious." The repetition of the word brings strength and power to the lines and creates a chantlike effect. The dactyl is used in the first phrase of each line, as in "Glorious the northern lights astream." The images are hurled at the reader: "the sun in mid-career," "the assembled fires," "the comet's train," "the almighty stretch'd-out arm," "th' enraptured main"—all glorious. Stupendous as are these natural wonders, however, says the poet, equally glorious are the human "hosannas from the den," and "the catholidc amen." In the last line of LXXXV, the second stanza of the trio, Smart anticipates the introduction of Christ in the final stanza by asserting, "Glorious the martyr's gore."[42]

Smart speaks to God in the final stanza (LXXXVI) and declares that most glorious of all is "the crown/Of Him that brought salvation down/ By meekness, call'd thy Son." After stressing David's faith, his gratitude, and his spiritual response to the wonders of the world, Smart has come at last to David's salvation, his link to Christ. In the final three lines the poet identifies with David and speaks of his own role in plotting the *Song.* Through God's belief in him, says Smart, his "matchless deed," his poem, was "DETERMINED, DARED, and Done." This final alliterative line halts the poem with emphasis and meaning; some of the phrasing may derive from an apocalyptic passage of Daniel XI: "For that which is determined shall be done."

Brittain has remarked, "In this final summary of the character of the poet-king, Smart stresses those elements of the religious life which were to him the sum of it all: David's gratitude, his faith, his prayer, his pure heart, and his salvation through Christ. . . . In this poem, as in most great works of art, the real subject is the author. Smart has an intense religious experience, and this poem is his most triumphal expression of it."[43]

XVII   *The* Song *and Its Poet*

Smart indeed revealed much of himself in his glorification of David's supreme adoration of God. The poet ignored almost entirely, however, several other themes found in the Psalms; for example, many lines speak of the comfort and protection David found in God, an important auxiliary theme of praise. From even the early Psalms, David's voice may be heard: "Hear me when I call, O God of my righteousness;/ Thou hast enlarged me when I was in distress" (IV); "The Lord also will be a refuge from the oppressed" (IX); "The Lord is my shepherd; I shall not want" (XXIII); "I cried unto thee, and thou hast healed me"(XXX); "God is our refuge and strength,/ A very present help in trouble"(XLVI). Yet David sometimes cries out in accusing questions: "My God, my God, why hast thou forsaken me?/ Why art thou so far from helping me, and from the words of my roaring?(XXIV)"

In his *Song,* Smart neither seeks protection from God nor questions God's will. The poet is totally committed to his basic philosophy that all creations of God are manifestations of God's love and that it is man's duty and privilege to adore Him. There is not a self-seeking or querulous note in the *Song*. The tone is of pure joy, exultant in contemplation of God's mercy. Smart, despite a life of few triumphs and many tragedies, retained the child's uncritical gift of wonder at the beauty and variety of the world. Nothing that happened to him could mar the greatness and goodness he saw in God and in God's works.

Of the *Song* and its poet, Devlin has stated: "Only genius could make pure goodness as piercingly attractive as Smart has done. One could go on endlessly trying to analyze the flash-points of his genius—the interplay of concrete and abstract, natural and artifact, exotic and familiar—and so on. But to me, it is more relevant to point out that all the best and sanest in Smart went to the making of this poem: his 'Franciscan' love of God and God's creatures; his scholarship and meditative reading; his happy childhood and boyhood; his happy (while it lasted) marriage and parenthood; and the acutely sensitive and subjective images which he retained of these happy experiences."[44]

CHAPTER 6

The Last Works of Christopher Smart

I Poems, *1763*

Although the reception of *A Song to David,* published in April, 1763, a few months after Smart's release, was not very favorable, the poet continued his efforts to become again a part of London's literary scene. In July of the same year he published *Poems,* containing *Reason and Imagination,* a fable dedicated to his old enemy but now friend, Kenrick. The volume also contained two odes, one addressed to General Draper and the other to Admiral Pocock, as well as "An Epistle to John Sherratt, Esq."

Because of its biographical content, the "Epistle to John Sherratt" is of some interest, as Sherratt seems to have been responsible for Smart's release. Smart explains, "Well nigh seven years had fill'd their tale,/ . . . And Found no friend to grief and *Smart,*/ Like Thee and Her, thy sweeter part." To Sherratt, Smart exclaims, " 'Tis you that have in my behalf,/ Produced the robe and kill'd the calf;/ Have hail'd the *restoration* day." That Sherratt met some opposition in his efforts appears likely. For Smart says of Sherratt's deed, "Whose spirit open and avow'd/ Arrayed itself against the crowd." The spirit of gratitude—always an important virtue to Smart—infuses the entire poem.

In *Reason and Imagination,* Smart again sets the natural against the cultivated. Imagination is depicted as a beautiful lady adorning herself in her chamber: "Upon her hair, with brilliants graced,/ Her tower of beamy gold she plac'd." On her breast, a verse wrought in gems says, "I make and shift the scenes of thought." In her right hand, she holds a magic wand; in her left, a chart "With figures far surpassing art." Reason, in contrast, dwells in a little cottage and applies himself to the

103

Book of Wisdom. Imagination tells Reason that he is much too grave, too much a slave and that she can lead him from "this hole and ditch/ To gay Conception's top-most pitch." Reason is further tempted by the lady's sensuous language: "I'll bring you to the pearly cars,/ By dragons drawn, above the stars." Reason tells Imagination that he cannot take her for a mate, but that, "whenso'er your raptures rise,/ I'll try to come with my supplies."

Together they will wage war on dullness; and, when Imagination makes a sally, Reason must be there "for conduct's sake." But, in the last part of the fable, Smart turns to Kenrick and tells him not to allow his "fondness for the sage" to decoy him from "The Book of Sempiternal Bliss." For in the Bible, says the poet, may be found wisdom beyond man's imagination and reason: "The truth to full perfection brought,/ Beyond the sage's deepest thought;/ Beyond the poet's highest flight."

II   *Intermediate Publications*

Another slim volume of verse, *Poems on Several Occasions,* which contains *Munificence and Modesty,* appeared in November, 1763. Smart described the book as "A little Miscellany that has been honoured with the approbation of the first names of the Literary World." *Munificence and Modesty* he called, "A Poem; The Hint from a Painting of Guido." Devlin suggests that the painting referred to is probably *The Coronation of the Virgin,* by Guido Reni, which depicts Mary as a peasant girl being crowned by a group of angels.

Devlin also points out that Smart made an attempt to treat the girl in the poem as simply Modesty refusing Munificence for a simpler life—not as Mary. But there are echoes of the Virgin in lines such as these: "A name that no distraction knows,/ Whose fragrance is as SHARON'S rose," and "Yet, yet accept a gift of love,/ The royal Sceptre and the Dove." Especially in the last movement of the poem, when "The vast Cherubic flight" of angels crown the maiden, the poet's real intention seems evident in the lines: ". . . Lo! this is SHE,/ Which has achieved the first degree." Perhaps Smart, suggests Devlin, for fear of being accused of "popery" was unable to clearly identify Modesty.[1] In April, 1764, appeared his oratorio *Hannah.*

Smart brought out another little volume of poems, *Ode to the Earl of Northumberland . . . With Some Other Pieces,* in July, 1764. The title piece, which celebrates the Earl of Northumberland's being appointed Lord Lieutenant of Ireland, is dull and pedestrian; and the remarks of the *Critical Review* seem apropos: "Mr. Smart informs us, in the advertisement prefixed to this poem, that the excellent person to whom it is addressed was so far from approving of the printing it, that he gave pious injunctions to the contrary. We shall add, that this was a proof not only of the noble lord's modesty, but of his taste and good sense."[2] Devlin sees a foreshadowing of Wordsworth in one of the finer lyrics in the work, "On a Bed of Guernsey Lilies." The lines run, "Lo thro' her gay nature grieves,/ How brief she is and frail,/ . . . Yet still the philosophic mind/ Consolatory food can find." The last three lines have a poignant beauty: "We never are deserted quite;/ 'Tis by succession of delight/ That love supports his reign."

Smart's last and most ambitious effort of the year was *A Poetical Translation of the Fables of Phaedrus,* mentioned in the *Public Advertiser* on December 17, 1764. The original Latin and the translation were printed on opposite pages. Included also were the Appendix of Gudius and a parsing index for students. Smart dedicated this volume to young Master Delaval and spoke of the favors he had received from his "amiable and excellent parents." This translation, commissioned by Dodsley, did nothing to add to Smart's literary reputation; but it did secure him some ready money which he badly needed.

III   *A Translation of the Psalms and Hymns*

During the period when the above-mentioned works appeared, Smart continued his efforts to publish his long-promised translation of the Psalms. Some of his musical friends rallied to his rescue, and in October, 1765, there appeared a collection of melodies by well-known organists, including Dr. Nares, Composer and Master of the Children of his Majesty's Chapel Royal; and an old college friend of the poet, John Randall, now music professor and organist of King's Chapel, Cambridge. *A Collection of Melodies for the Psalms of David According to the Version of Christopher Smart, A.M. By the most eminent Composers of Church Music,* included thirty pages of music and text. Each hymn was identified with the name of the composer.

The announcement of the coming publication of the *Collection,* points out Devlin, was "not only a splendid advertisement; it was a sort of pledge (though in the event an unfulfilled one) that the version would be used in Church services and so command a good sale."[3] The promise inherent in this forerunner to the entire collection encouraged the distinguished printer Dryden Leach to accept the task of printing the contemplated whole of Smart's translation of the Psalms. Thus the long-awaited *A Translation of the Psalms of David* appeared, with the addition of "a poem beyond what was promised in the Proposals"—*A Song to David*. The translation evidently appeared in August, 1765, as promised in the *General Advertiser*, for criticism of the translation appears in the September magazine.

While it is difficult to see the verse paraphrase of the Psalms as much beyond preparation—but a valuable one—for the poet's writing of *A Song to David*, Smart's *Hymns and Spiritual Songs* (1765) should be included in his most noteworthy verse. Of these hymns Devlin has said, "the best of his hymns have a quality all their own, austerely tender, as if the baroque had developed gently and easily from the medieval, skipping the doubt and passion and the grandeur that lay between, or as if Abelard's Latin had quite effortlessly become English, taking only a polish from the classics on the way."[4]

The hymn on the nativity, for example, contains some especially lovely lines: "Nature'd decorations glisten/ Far above their usual trim; . . . Whiter blossoms burst untimely/ On the blest Mosaic thorn." The last stanza of the hymn has a dignified simplicity: "God all-bounteous, all-creative,/ Whom no ills from good dissuade,/ Is incarnate, and a native/ Of the very world he made."

Hymn XIII, to St. Philip and St. James, also includes some notable lines: "Hark, aloud, the black-bird whistles,/ With surrounding fragrance blest,/ And the goldfinch in the thistles/ Makes provision for her nest." Here, as in *A Song to David*, Smart speaks of all aspects of nature: ". . . the painted beauties thicken/ Colour'd by the master's hand," and ". . . the rocks supply the coney/ With a fortress and an home." Smart was not able, however, to maintain a consistent quality throughout his hymns; and some of them—as Devlin puts it—"plunge into heated doggerel."[5] This critic also points to the anti-Romanism which mars some of Smart's patriotic hymns which were intended for the civic feasts of the Church of England.

IV   *Smart's Verse Translation of Horace*

Smart continued to work, and in 1767 appeared his verse translation of Horace, together with the important critical Preface to it. His reason for writing the verse translation seems to have been to supersede the prose one, which he thought would hurt his memory. In the Preface, however, the poet states that he—like Horace—wrote because he needed the money. Especially valuable are Smart's remarks concerning the features of Horace's poetry and his own efforts to preserve "the lucky risk of the Horation boldness" in English. Brittain provides a thorough discussion of Smart's remarks on Horace in his Introduction to *Poems of Christopher Smart,* and it is this critic's account and analysis of these remarks which follows.

Smart explains that "Horace is not so much an original in respect to his matter and sentiments (which are rather too frequently borrowed), as with regard to that unrivalled peculiarity of expression which has excited the admiration of all succeeding ages." By way of explaining the features of Horace's poetry which account for this "peculiarity of expression," Smart remarks: "In the first place I have especially attended to, what the critics call his *curiosa felicitas,* of which many of my predecessors seem not to have entertained the most remote idea. . . . In truth this is a beauty, that occurs rather in the Odes, than the other parts of Horace's works; where the aiming at familiarity of style excluded the curiosity of choice diction."[6] Smart then gives several instances in his own translation where he feels he has been able to bring this stylistic quality into English.

Smart mentions some of Horace's advice concerning diction—advice the eighteenth-century poet occasionally followed. Horace permitted the use of old words; Smart translated Horace's dictum in prose: "Sundry words shall revive which now have receded." Smart also revived obsolete words; indeed, his later poetry is full of archaic language. Horace also allowed the coinage of new words, if used in moderation, and the use of a word in an unusual order. Smart did not coin an unusually large number of new words, but he did follow Horace's precepts concerning the use of an unusual word, or of a common word in an unusual sense. Horace's remarks of the subject were translated as follows: " 'Tis arduous common things to say/ In such a clean peculiar way/ Until they fairly seem your own."[7] Brittain comments, "Smart was, I believe, quite conscious of this difficulty, but it seems to me that much of the strangeness of his verse is due to his sincere effort to find a 'clean peculiar way' of giving expression to his material."[8]

The verse translation itself was published in a four-volume edition with the Latin and English versions on opposite pages. This edition, dedicated to Sir Francis Blake Delaval, has never been reprinted and is rarely found today. Of the verse translation Brittain has said, "To anyone interested in neo-classic poetry, the entire translation is worth serious study, both for its faults and its many virtues."[9] This critic denies that Smart's early prose translation of Horace ever hurt the poet's memory; and he asserts that, if the verse translation were equally well known, the poet's reputation would suffer even less.

V   The Parables *and* Abimelech

From Smart's verse translation of Horace, he turned to a work designed for children: *The Parables of Our Lord and Saviour Jesus Christ.* The *Parables,* published in 1768, were dedicated to three-year-old Bonnell Thornton. In his dedication Smart writes, "There are Sundry Instances of our Blessed Saviour's fondness for Children, as a Man; and He has assured us, we can have no Part in Him without imitating their Innocence and Simplicity." In this spirit Smart rendered in verse seventy-three of the parables of Christ and other biblical scenes, done in octosyllabic couplets—over three thousand lines.

"The Barren Fig-Tree" illustrates the clarity and simplicity with which Smart tells the story of the parable and makes his moral point. Though the fig tree bears not a single fruit, it is not destroyed because of the pleading of the gardener: ". . . Lord, I implore,/ Till I shall dig about the root." Thus, says the poet, God in his justice must cut off each sinful man; but mercy—through Christ—intercedes for him. As year after year passes, says the poet, "Perhaps the wretch, through love or fear,/ Himself to grace may recommend."

Among the biblical events included in the group of parables is the story of Martha and Mary, which Smart calls, "Martha reproved." After telling the story, Smart states his moral: *"All worldly work and carnal cares/ Are little to the soul's affairs:/ . . . No.—Ghostly toil and mental pain,/ For bless incorruptible gain,/ Are that which Christ our hope desires."* Another poem, "Our Saviour washing his Disciples Feet," celebrates the event and closes with an admonition very close to the heart of the poet: *"From thence all Christians should deduce,/ That brother brother should attend/ As kind assistant, guide, and friend/ . . . Respect the pattern set on high/ And learn of CHRIST to live and die."*

In the same year (1768) Smart published the oratorio *Abimelech,* which was performed at the Theatre-Royal in Covent Garden. A mediocre piece, it was probably written to augment Smart's very meager funds. It is noteworthy that this oratorio is the only work of the poet's last few years written for an adult audience. The poet's *Parables* were intended, as was his last volume, *Hymns for the Amusement of Children,* for children.[10]

<h3 style="text-align:center">VI   Hymns for the Amusement of Children</h3>

Hymns for the Amusement of Children, a less pedestrian work than the *Parables,* appears to have been written after Smart was confined to the King's Bench Prison for debt. The little duodecimo volume was published in 1770 without Smart's name—probably to avoid the poet's creditors—by his brother-in-law, Thomas Carnan. It was popular enough to run through three English editions in five years, but no copy of the first two editions exists today. Only one copy of the third edition, dated 1775, is known to survive; this volume is preserved in the Bodleian at Oxford. An American edition, dated 1791, at Philadelphia, bears the following inscription: "By the Rev. Christopher Smart"; only one copy of this edition has been found. In 1947 Blackwell published a facsimile edition, with an introduction by Edmund Blunden.

Smart dedicated his volume to "His Royal Highness, Prince Frederick,/ Bishop of Osnaburg," and there is a likeness of the little prince as a frontispiece. Especially attractive are the quaint woodcuts, one above each hymn, illustrating the theme. The titles of the hymns concern some of the qualities the poet had long admired: "Faith," "Hope," "Charity," "Justice," and "Mercy," among others. He also wrote several companion pieces: "Mirth" and "Melancholy," "At Dressing in the Morning" and "At Undressing in the Evening," and others.

In these hymns for children, the poet underlines his favorite themes. For example, in "Hope" Smart addresses Hannah—a symbolic figure to the poet, for his first oratorio celebrated her career—and tells her not to despair, but "Quick to the Tabernacle speed;/ There on thy knees prefer thy pray'r." Because of her prayer, Hannah's hope was made manifest in the birth of Samuel. Hymn XVIII, "Prayer," echoes old rules of life for the poet himself: "Pray without ceasing (says the Saint)/ . . . With grace the bloom, and faith the root,/ The pray'r shall bring eternal fruit." The first two lines of "Watching" repeat once more

Smart's frequent admonition to pray: "At every tempter's first essay,/ Be sure to watch, be sure to pray."

Smart again relates man's need to pray and man's need to praise God in gratitude for his many blessings. There is a suggestion of the great "Adoration" stanzas of the *Song* in the hymn entitled "Generosity," a muted but still fervent note. The first stanza speaks of God's "stupendous generosity." The next stanza shows the poet going—as he so often does—to nature to make his point: "Not for themselves the bees prepare/ Their honey, and the fleecy care,/ Not for themselves are shorn." Stanza III celebrates the crucifixion: "The Lord shed on the Holy Rood/ His infinitely generous blood,/ Not for himself, but all." After commenting on Christ's sacrifice for man, the poet asks, "Then who can praise, and love and fear/ Enough?—since he himself, 'tis clear,/ Is also gratitude." In "Gratitude," the poet bids the children not to be afraid of God—not to be like "Adam trembling"—but to think of God as "the lover/ Of mankind, restor'd and free."

Smart, who felt a kinship with all living creatures, again asks for kindness in "Good Nature to Animals"; but he gives his own peculiar turn to the admonition: "Nor let neglected Dormice sleep/ To death beneath thy wool." But Smart also felt a kinship with man, and the theme of the brotherhood of man runs through his work. His lines in "Honesty" make a promise: "To give my brother more than due,/ In talent or in name;/ Nor e'en mine enemy pursue." He resolves to go beyond mere forgiveness to the enemy: "Nay more, to bless him and to pray,/ And give the wages of the day/ To him that hunts my soul." [i.e., The warden]

Smart often spoke of the beauty of charity, and in the hymn of that name he implores in a childlike way: "Then guide, O Christ, this little hand,/ To deal thy bounties round the land;/ To clothe and feed the hungry poor." One of his last hymns, "Pray Remember the Poor," relates an experience: "I JUST came by the prison-door,/ I gave a penny to the poor." Smart himself tried to help the poor in the prison where he lived. To him "Humanity's a charming thing" as he writes in his hymn entitled "Learning." And, while the poet is often criticized for paying homage to the rich and distinguished, his love for humanity was not reserved for the notable of the world; it spread to all men.

This little group of hymns, written in four, five, or six-line stanzas, are Smart's last poetic expression. The lines have an alternating rhyme scheme or are in couplets. Brittain has called the volume the poet's "final word upon the meaning of religion."[11] The critic points out that the poems are not technically striking or complex—that their phrases, rhythms, and structural patterns are, for the most part, simple. Brittain then observes: "It is rather the spirit of this little book that is important. The sonorous grandeur of *A Song to David* is not here; neither is the assertive brilliance of some of the *Hymns and Spiritual Songs* or the mystic fervor of others. This last book is written in a mood of resignation and quiet peace.... It should be remembered always in judging these last verses of Smart that they were written for children.... There is in some of them an apparent artlessness, a simplicity of diction combined with the most startlingly accurate arrangement of thought which gives them a quality very like that of *Songs of Innocence and Experience.*"[12]

CHAPTER 7

Christopher Smart and the Critics

Christopher Smart's work was the subject of both favorable and unfavorable criticism during his lifetime and for a short time afterward. Most of this criticism was derogatory, partly because the poet's life and work became related in the public eye—to the detriment of the reputation of both—and partly because of the intellectual climate of the eighteenth century. Some of the Romantic attitudes of the nineteenth century were more favorable, however, to Smart; and a slow but intermittent revival of interest in his work began in this period. This interest has steadily increased because of new findings and wider and more objective criticism of Smart's work. Today his reputation stands on firm ground.

I Cambridge and Preconfinement Period in London

While at Cambridge, Christopher Smart had established himself as a person of scholarly and poetic ability. He had been honored with academic posts at the university, had translated Pope's *Ode For Music on St. Cecilia's Day*—for which he had received a commendatory letter from Pope—and had written some Latin verses. In addition, he had experimented in a variety of poetic forms popular in his day. His decision to seek a literary career in London, therefore, was founded on some previous encouragement and success.

Smart's work during the preconfinement period in London was received with some favor because it corresponded to the spirit and form of the era. The five Seatonian poems, the *Poems on Several Occasions* of 1752, the *Hilliad,* and the contributions to the *Student* and *Midwife* held this appeal and demonstrated his proficiency in almost any kind of verse he attempted; his faithfulness to neo-Classic principles also made his work quite acceptable to his audience. These pieces, Bond observes, were highly derivative, despite some "flashes of real poetic fire." Smart's reputation during this period, Bond suggests, was "more for ability and promise than for solid achievement."[1]

One of Smart's most derogatory critics during this period was William Kenrick, with whom Smart became involved in one of the many Grub Street quarrels of the day. Smart, however, was able to offset this kind of criticism partly by retaliatory remarks as well as by praise of his own work in *The Midwife.*

Some of the reviewers of Smart's work both commended the writing and deplored certain aspects of it. For example, concerning Smart's occasional prologue and epilogue to *Othello*—written at the request of John Delaval— a letter signed "B. C." in the *Gentleman's Magazine* (March, 1751) had this to say: "I wish the world had not known that this prologue and epilogue were written by a gentleman, who has hitherto been esteem'd a genius and a scholar . . . it is hoped that he will consider before it is too late, that genius and learning, prostituted to such service, must at length lose their dignity, and be regarded only as the tools of those who hire them for use."[2]

Marked with the same mixed attitude was John Hill's discussion of Smart's *Poems on Several Occasions* appearing in the *Monthly Review* (August, 1752). Hill commented that Smart was "with Gray and Mason, with the first of the present age in spirit, in fire, and true poetic genius"; but he informed Smart that his genius was "in need of formation," and be warned the poet in closing "to be more attentive to the finishing of his works for the future."[3] A number of bitter exchanges between Hill and Smart followed.

While echoes of the quarrel between Smart and Hill continued to be heard on Grub Street, the violence of the affair dissipated itself as Smart continued to work. His Seatonian prize poem, *On the Power of the Supreme Being,* appeared toward the close of December, 1753, and was praised by the *Gentleman's Magazine* (January, 1754), which printed an extract from it. The same magazine, in announcing the winner of the poem award in 1754 to be George Bally, made this observation: "This prize has for many years been constantly assigned to the ingenious Mr. Smart, who was not this year among the competitors."[4] Except for the Seatonian prize poems, Smart wrote little of note in the period between 1753 and 1756. In 1756 he published his prose translation of Horace, which was a great success, continuing to be published and used both in England and America.

Thus before Smart's confinement the poet had some reputation for scholarship; he had made some important and influential friends who helped to spread word concerning his writing. And his work itself, while not of great distinction, was in bulk and variety enough to make him a significant part of the literary scene. The orthodoxy of his production, with its flashes of vivid and arresting lines, appealed to many who considered him a promising young poet. From 1756 to 1763, however, he was generally inactive in literary circles because of his confinement; but his friends did visit him during this period, helping him to keep in touch, to some extent, with the outside world. It is now known that Smart wrote *Jubilate Agno* during this period, but the work was never published during the poet's lifetime and was probably not generally known.

II *From Release to Death (1763-1771)*

Smart wrote industriously after his release from the asylum in 1763 until his death in 1771; but, as Bond has pointed out, "The critical response was discouraging, as indeed it was for all his later works. His friends were too ready to be saddened, and his enemies too eager to be pleased, by discovering signs of madness in everything he did."[5] Smart's quarrels with the critics made it almost impossible for him to get fair reviews, and he was consequently unable to sell his work. Most readers seemed to share Mason's opinion that the *Song* proved Smart as mad as ever, and this attitude influenced the reception of Smart's later writing.

A typical example of the reception accorded Smart's later work is discernible in a review prompted by a heated exchange between the poet and the magazine. The *Critical Review* (November, 1763) commented concerning a volume of poems containing *Munificence and Modesty* and published during the latter part of 1763: "We wish, from a regard to the reputation of Mr. Smart, who formerly made a considerable figure in the world of literature, that they had been suppressed, as they can do him no honour."[6] The *Review* then spoke of Smart's "departed muse."

The *Monthly Review* (April, 1763), in referring to Smart's later work, also alluded to the poet's madness and implied that his genius had departed. This magazine had helped to circulate the story that the poet had scratched the *Song* on the wainscot of his madhouse cell. Of the *Song* the *Monthly* had rather generously commented, "From the sufferings of this ingenious gentleman, we could not but expect the performance before us to be greatly irregular; but we shall certainly characterize it more justly, we call it irregularly great."[7] But the *Monthly* (September, 1763) was more unkind in its review of the *Reason and Imagination* quarto. The critic would not enter any discussion concerning the merits of the poems; he would simply quote a few applicable lines from Milton's *Sampson:* " 'O change beyond report, thought, or belief!/ . . . By how much from the top of wondrous glory/ To lowest pitch of abject fortune art thou fall'n.' "[8] The *Monthly* barely mentioned Smart's translation of the *Psalms;* and of his versified *Parables*—one of his last publications—its reviewer wrote scathingly that the dedication of the pieces to three-year-old George Thornton was particularly appropriate.

Smart retained some loyal friends but continued to suffer adverse criticism until the end. In her diary, Fanny Burney denounced "The Critical Reviewers, ever eager to catch at every opportunity of lessening and degrading the merit of this unfortunate man."[9] But the *Critical Review,* the *Monthly,* and other publications only reflected the general opinion of the time: Smart had shown genius and promise during the early part of his career, but his work after his release from the madhouse could not be taken seriously because of its strange, imaginative, and unorthodox quality.

III   The Poems *(1791)* to Browning's Parleyings

There were those who tried to keep the poet's memory alive, however, and in 1791—twenty years after Smart's death—appeared *The Poems of the Late Christopher Smart,* a two-volume edition prefixed with an account of the poet's life and writings by his nephew, Christopher Hunter. While Hunter omitted most of Smart's later work, he did include some of the poet's early poems not previously identified. Because Smart wrote under a number of different pseudonyms, the identifying of these poems by Hunter has been a great help to scholars. The *Monthly Review* gave a quite generous appraisal of the volume.

Little was heard of Smart's work following this edition until 1794 when Robert Anderson included some of his poems in *The Works of the British Poets.* In 1810, Chalmers included some of Smart's poetry in his *The Works of the English Poets,* together with a biographical and critical introduction. Chalmers, like Anderson, did not reprint the *Song;*

but he commented upon it: "There are some passages of more majestic animation than in any of his former pieces, and others in which the expression is mean, and the sentiments unworthy of the poet or subject."[10] Chalmers spoke favorably of Smart's religious poetry, especially *Hymn to the Supreme Being;* but he thought that Smart was at his best in his lighter verse.

During this period the *Song* was neglected, but in 1814 an article in the *Quarterly Review* revived interest in the poem. The writer regretted the omission of the *Song* in Anderson and Chalmers because the circumstances under which the poem was supposedly written— composed in a madhouse, the lines indented with a key upon the wainscot—appealed to the Romantic turn of mind: "The loss of such a poem composed under such circumstances, by a man of such talents is greatly to be regretted."[11] The critic also used such terms as "strength," "feeling," and "animation" in reference to the poem, words giving the *Song* Romantic overtones. To show these qualities, he quoted a few stanzas of the *Song.* In 1818, when the entire *Song* was reprinted, the *Gentleman's Magazine* commented favorably concerning it. Other periodicals reviewed the *Song* and selected particular lines, phrases, and words for special comment. The legend of its composition was repeated.

There was a short revival of interest in Smart, but it soon died. In 1825 Mrs. Le Noir, the poet's daughter, wrote an appreciation of her father and his work which she prefixed to an edition of her own poems. In 1827 the *Song* was published again, but Smart's name seldom occurred in any serious discussion of poetry. He was a kind of literary curiosity. Many critics seemed to share Leigh Hunt's opinion: "This . . . reminds me . . . of poor Kit Smart, in whom a good deal of real genius seems to have wasted itself away in complexional weakness."[12]

But Smart's name occasionally appeared in literary history, and several editions of his own writings were published before he appeared in Browning's *Parleyings* in 1887. His name was mentioned, of course, in Boswell's *Life of Johnson,* and in the letters and diaries of his contemporaries. Isaac Disraeli discussed Smart briefly in his *Quarrels of Authors* (1881). The poet's prose translation of Horace and the *Fables of Phaedrus* were republished several times in the nineteenth century. The reprinting of the *Song* at various times during the period helped to make this poem familiar to many readers. George Gilfallan, who reprinted the *Song* in his *Specimens with Memoirs of Less-Known*

British Poets (1860), called the poet "Single-Poem Smart"; but his discussion of the *Song* was very favorable: "Incoherence and extravagance we find here and there; but it is not the flutter of weakness, it is the fury of power . . . . Indeed, there are portions of the 'Song to David' which a Milton or a Shakespeare has never surpassed."[13]

An early indication of the modern view of Smart—which finds distinction in much of the poet's work—was A. C. Ward's note in the *Antiquarian* (1885). The critic did not accept Gilfallan's appelation, "Single-Poem Smart." While the *Song* might be Smart's best piece, he remarked, the poet had written enough to fill two volumes, much of it very good. Concerning the poet, Ward wrote: "He has a fine command of the English language, wit, ingenuity, and an ear for rhythm; but a good deal of sameness runs through all his writings."[14]

IV *Browning's* Parleyings *and Late Nineteenth-Century Comment*

Although Christopher Smart had a limited literary reputation in the years after his death, it was his appearance in Browning's *Parleyings with Certain People of Importance in Their Day* which aroused a sustained revival of interest in his work. Published in 1887, Browning's poem, "With Christopher Smart," awakened a great deal of interest in the *Song,* besides enhancing Smart's literary reputation. In the poem, Browning coupled Smart with Milton and Keats; and he declared: "Smart, solely of such songmen, pierced the screen/ 'Twixt thing and word, lit language straight from soul." In a letter Browning mentioned that he had repeated some stanzas of the *Song* to well-known people: "Tennyson, the present Bishop of London, and, last year to Wendell Holmes, who had asked me innocently at Oxford, 'whether I knew the wonderful poem.' Weak passages there undoubtedly are, but the strong ones are decisive as to Smart's power and right of place."[15] A review of Browning's volume quotes Dante Gabriel Rossetti as saying of the *Song:* "This wonderful poem of Smart's is the only great *accomplished* poem of the last century . . . . A masterpiece of rich imagery, exhaustive resources, and reverbrant sound."[16]

One of the first pieces to follow Browning's *Parleyings* was Edmund Gosse's *Gossip in a Library,* published in 1891, which devotes some attention to the *Song* but finds praiseworthy lines in some of Smart's other poems; Gosse had previously published some biographical material on Smart in the *Athenaeum* (1887). When an entry for Christopher Smart by Thomas Seccombe was published in the *Dictionary of National Biography* (1897), the material included some critical remarks about Smart's work and was influential in the early study of the poet's whole canon.

V   *Twentieth-Century Editions and Bibliography*

The revival of interest in Smart that continued into the twentieth century included a reexamination of not only the *Song,* but also Smart's other works. For as long as he was known as "Single-Poem Smart," the poet could be only of limited interest. A number of publications were influential in making Smart's entire body of works better known, although the task of gathering the material was made more difficult because of Smart's habit of using pseudonyms. A work of major importance in establishing Smart's canon was G. J. Gray's bibliography in 1903.

This work has been cited by Callan as the definitive account of Smart's work, the only important addition being *Jubilate Agno,* a manuscript which was written, as has been noted, while Smart was confined and which was discovered in 1937 by William Force Stead. Stead added a thirty-nine-page introduction and notes to the manuscript when he published it in 1939 as *Rejoice in the Lamb, A Song from Bedlam.* Stead's exhaustive scholarship did much to increase the interest already generated in Smart, although Stead saw the *Jubilate* as "a strange, chaotic composition," of value because of its biographical references and indications of sources for *A Song to David.*[17]

Valuable to the student wanting to survey the bulk of Smart's poetry is Callan's two-volume edition of Smart's work, published in 1949. This edition, which contains all of Smart's clearly identified poetry, excludes the translations of Horace and Phaedrus, the libretti of *Hannah* and *Abimelech,* and the Latin poems. Another volume, *Poems by Christopher Smart,* edited by Robert Brittain and published in 1950, contains only a partial selection of Smart's poem; it includes some of Smart's verse translations, some poems not included in the Callan edition, and more copious notes. A new edition of *Jubilate Agno,* edited by W. H. Bond, was published in 1954.

VI   *Twentieth-Century Scholarship and Criticism*

With the increased notice which Smart's total production has received—as a result of new discoveries and editions of his work—a new type of criticism has appeared. Peter Davis has commented concerning modern appraisal of Smart: "a new and more thorough type of criticism . . . . is apparent in the trend of comment since Browning, which, in contrast to the generalities of earlier writers, points out specifics in spirit and construction of the *Song* and other works of Smart."[18] Davis observes the increased inclusion of Smart in literary histories and anthologies.

Some of the criticism about specifics concern Smart's prosody. George Saintsbury, in his *History of English Prosody* (1908), was one of the first to analyze the prosody of Smart's poetry. After devoting some study to the six-line stanza of the *Song,* he commented: "Its movement is of the most various and minutely divided character, and yet it is perfectly symphonic and continuous as a whole."[19] Thomas Seccombe's *Age of Johnson* (1914) included another examination of Smart's prosody; Seccombe pointed out some similarities between Smart and Blake. Eric Partridge also linked Blake and Smart in subject matter and lyrical quality of poetic line. Partridge remarked of the six-line stanza of the *Song:* "Smart handles the measure, which in lesser men tends to jog-trot, with great force and dignity; and he rimes very ably."[20]

In 1925 appeared a critical biography by K. A. McKenzie, *Christopher Smart: sa vie et ses oeuvres,* published in Paris and commenting on the *Song* as well as on Smart's other works. When Edith Sitwell reprinted the *Song* in her *Pleasures of Poetry* (1930), she remarked about the "extreme strangeness of the imagery; all natural objects are seen with such clarity that, for the moment, nothing else exists." Of particular lines which she quotes, she comments: "There is a curious modernity, as well as beauty, which is both ancient and eternal, in the . . . lines"; furthermore, "All the verses dealing with adoration have, to my mind, a deep and eternal beauty; never were flowers and fruit seen more clearly, or with more love; never were all living creatures more welcomed into God's love."[21]

Other critics of the modern period also gave some attention to the *Song* but did not neglect Smart's other poetry. John Middleton Murray in *Discoveries* (1924) praised the unity of the *Song* and also admired the *Hymns and Spiritual Songs.* In his *Concise Cambridge History* (1941), George Sampson spoke of Smart's fables and "lighter pieces in a Hudibrastic or Swiftian vein" as being admirable. Sampson saw Smart as anticipating Blake in some of the lines from *Rejoice in the Lamb* (Stead's edition of *Jubilate Agno*).

A valuable addition to the critical material on Smart is Edmund Blunden's biographical and critical preface to his edition of *A Song to David* with other poems. Blunden suggested in his preface that some of Smart's poems other than the *Song* might be valuable because the "glorious music and painting" of the *Song* demands that anything throwing light on its writer should be revived. Blunden regarded these poems mainly as illuminations of the *Song*. Of the *Song* Blunden remarks: "Its daring rapture, glowing picture, rich and rare words, chime and answer of stanza are beyond dispute; its perfections are rose-marks. The splendor seems Hebraic in origin, but the soil, the sun and rain of the poem are English. There is much speed, such definition in the making of the verse as to stamp the stanza form, though many have used it, Christopher Smart's."[22]

In 1934 appeared Lawrence Binyon's *The Case of Christopher Smart,* a short but distinguished treatment of the *Song* with observations concerning Smart as a poet. Binyon suggests that what gives the *Song* its peculiar character is that, while the plan of the poem is "methodical and deliberate, the general effect is one of excitement and a certain incoherence, like the sudden shiftings of a kaleidoscope." The critic notes the freshness in the rhyme sounds—unlike, he comments, the school of Pope, which preferred common rhymes. While the rhythm is plain and without subtleties, says Binyon, the character of the stanza does not lend itself to subtle rhythm. Binyon explains: "the poem, with all its sudden transitions, has such momentum that it seems to gather speed as it goes, and one cannot think of another form of stanza which would better carry the theme."

Smart is not considered to be a mystic by Binyon; the poet, he thinks, had a transcendent God and his work is not symbolic. Perhaps, suggests Binyon, if Smart had been born in another century and under other influences, he might been a mystic. The sensuous quality in the *Song* sets it apart from the eighteenth century, a period which relied on reason, not on the senses, believes Binyon, and links the poet with the mystics to some degree: "this joy of the senses is in the *Song* drenched in religious feeling, in the mood of adoration. And in that mood he sees everything in nature glowing and distinct, as it glows in the mystic's vision."[23]

Rejoice in the Lamb received some attention from Edward Gay Ainsworth and Charles E. Noyes in their volume entitled *Christopher*

Smart, A Biographical and Critical Study (1943). They point out two themes as being responsible for some of the most enjoyable poetry in the manuscript: the first concerns the passage on the poet's cat Jeoffry, with its delightful description of the cat with metaphysical observation upon "the Cherub Cat"; the second theme relates to Smart's flowers, which, more than merely things of beauty to Smart, had many significances—"aesthetic, scientific, religious, medicinal, and mystic." But Ainsworth also devotes some attention to Smart's other work: the poet's early poems through the *Hymns for the Amusement of Children* are carefully and thoroughly examined, and many quotations show the poet's poetic genius and craftsmanship.

Ainsworth's discussion of the *Song* illumines many of the beauties of the poem and presents the plan and purpose of the piece. That Smart did not write anything as good as the *Song* before and nothing so good after makes it no difference, says Ainsworth—"by definition one does not surpass one's masterpiece. The *Song* . . . is a piece with his other religious verse—finer, sweeter, but of the same substance. There was no flame-transfigured moment when the god spoke through the tranced subject . . . say, rather, there was a moment of calm. Deep meditation, infinite concentration went into the Song."[24] Perhaps the critics' discussions of the *Song* are most valuable in showing Smart's talents, as Davis has suggested in "The Literary Reputation of Christopher Smart." But their survey of the poet's total production, biography, and much of his literary reputation—especially in his Grub Street days—makes this work by Ainsworth and Noyes a valuable and rewarding study.

Norman Callan's two-volume collection of Smart's poems (1949) supplies some critical comments from various sources and adds Callan's own penetrating interpretation of Smart. Callan notes that critics from Browning to Mr. Middleton Murray have singled out "A directness of expression, which makes no distinction between analogy and identity" as Smart's most noteworthy characteristic. But Smart's other merits, Callan suggests, should not be neglected. Smart has "intense perceptiveness, . . . is a poet with the eye of a painter developed to an unusually high degree. He has the stereoscopic vision which makes the object leap to the eye, the painter's sense of physical texture . . . . He is a miniaturist rather than a painter of broad effects."[25] Callan finds Smart's poetry full of "minute arabesques, which owe something of their manner to Pope." Smart's versatility should also be noted.

Bond, in his new edition of the *Jubilate* (1954), reorganized the text according to an antiphonal plan outlined in his introduction, and his additions to Stead's notes do much to dispel the idea of the manuscript as the chaotic product of a madman. Its plan, on the other hand, was orderly and rational, even though it broke down somewhat toward the end. Bond saw Smart as exhausted by the turmoil of Grub Street but as able in the seclusion of his confinement to work out a poetic theory and personal philosophy, to experiment with form and style in an original and unconventional manner. Of Smart, Bond remarks: "When he emerged from the shadows his days of limitation were over. Within a few months he published *A Song to David,* the mature product of his thought and labours."[26]

In 1961 two biographies with critical comment were published. Geoffrey Grigson's booklet, *Christopher Smart,* contains some brilliant remarks concerning Smart's early work as well as an interpretation of the *Song;* the *Song,* Grigson stresses, was no miracle without roots. The biography by Devlin, *Poor Kit Smart,* is an objective but sympathetic treatment of the poet. Devlin, who examines the whole canon of Smart's work, offers some excellent comments concerning the poet's motives and purposes. Devlin believes, with various other critics, that the popular picture of Smart as a continual drunkard is probably exaggerated; if Smart were constantly in such a state, asks Devlin, how was he able to produce such a large body of work?

Of articles concerning particular aspects of Smart's work, it may be said that there are not a great many, but that their number is increasing. Most of these articles discuss either *Jubilate Agno* or the *Song;* there is valuable work being done, however, on some of Smart's other writings. A few articles treat Smart's contributions to magazines; these articles occasionally offer additions—both of poetry and prose—to Smart's canon as described by Gray in his *Bibliography* of 1903. Most of the identifying of these additions is based on internal evidence, and the pieces are questioned by some scholars.

Smart's influence on modern poets is open to question. Several notable poets such as Edmund Blunden and Edith Sitwell have shown their appreciation of Smart by their critical remarks concerning his poetry and by their publishings of a *Song.* A very small group of contemporary poets who were questioned regarding an appraisal of Christopher Smart indicated that his writing had not, for the most part, been of much influence on their own writings, although several expressed admiration for his poetry. Marianne Moore wrote of the poet:

Christopher Smart's energy
                    originality
                    innate resourcefulness
                    in choice of diction
                    and rhythm

Make him one of my favorite poets.[27]

Richard Eberhart has remarked: "If I had encountered Smart first he might have influenced me but Blake got there first. So did Wordsworth. And later Hopkins meant more to me than Smart. Smart never influenced me but I gloried in him as a paeon-maker, a great celebrant, cataloguer and sender of revelations. He exemplified the notion that the mad are sane enough to see the truth."[28]

VII *Summary*

The regular collection of Christopher Smart's poetry, published in 1791 by Christopher Hunter, was of the ordinary eighteen-century tradition in neo-Classic attitudes toward literature, in forms such as the ode, and in techniques with Hudibrastic and Miltonic overtones. Lines of poetic fire and promise, however, can be observed throughout many of these poems and show that the poet's masterpiece, *A Song to David,* was not a sudden and solitary achievement. The poet began his use of the catalogue, his favorite structural device, in the Seaton poems, where he also began to develop his personal theology. From his versification of the Psalms and the early *Hymn,* he discovered that the lyric was best suited to his genius. The figures of David and Orpheus in his *Psalms* and *Jubilate Agno,* a madhouse manuscript only recently recovered, are identified with praise of an ordered and harmonic universe—the symbol of God's creative love. Within the *Jubilate,* a work with both Christian and Hebraic elements, are numerous references to science, music, nature, philosophy, and religion, notings which expressed attitudes formerly only tentatively extended.

In the *Song,* published soon after Smart's release from confinement, and excluded from the orthodox collection, Smart defined his religious philosophy in original and glowing terms. All things exist and move through God's love; the purpose of man, therefore, should be to joyfully praise and adore God. Smart's experiments in language and poetic structure, his inventiveness in getting variation in conventional rhythms, his exotic and sensuous imagery, all reach their most sublime form in this lyric. The superb technique, design, and diction of the *Song* lift the poem, as well as some of his other work, from the context of the eighteenth century. There is modern appeal in its intensity of feeling, complexity, and brilliance of execution. In philosophy and technique, Smart should be considered one of England's timeless, eminent religious poets.

Notes and References

Chapter One

1. This discussion derives much, in regard to organization and illustrative examples, from the account of the period in "The Eighteenth Century," *British Poetry and Prose,* ed. Paul Robert Lieder, Robert Morss Lovett, and Robert Kilburn Root (Boston, 1950), pp. 687-99.

Chapter Two

1. Quoted in Edward G. Ainsworth and Charles E. Noyes, *Christopher Smart: A Critical and Biographical Study,* no. 4 in *The University of Missouri Studies,* XVIII (Columbia, 1943), p. 8. Chapter I (pp. 8-15) supplies facts of Smart's early life.

2. *Ibid.,* p. 21. For the account of Smart's days at Cambridge, including the following listings of his library borrowings, I am indebted to Chapter II, pp. 16-35.

3. *Ibid.,* p. 41. Quoted from *The Nonpareil* (London, 1757), p. iii.

4. Christopher Hunter, "The Life of Christopher Smart," prefixed to *The Poems of Christopher Smart* (Reading, 1791), p. xxx.

5. Quoted in Christopher Devlin, *Poor Kit Smart* (London, 1961), p. 71.

6. *Ibid.,* pp. 71-72.

7. Quoted in Ainsworth and Noyes, *op. cit.,* p. 78.

8. *Ibid.,* p. 88.

9. *Ibid.,* p. 92.

10. *Ibid.,* p. 107.

11. Quoted in Devlin, *op. cit.,* pp. 162-64. Devlin reprints the entire letter and comments as I have indicated.

12. Robert E. Brittain, ed. *Poems by Christopher Smart* (Princeton, 1960), p. 48.

13. Devlin, *op. cit.*, p. 167.

14. *Ibid.*, p. 170.

15. Mme. Frances d' Arblay, *The Early Diary of Frances Burney*, ed. Annie Raine Ellis (London, 1889), vol. I, p. 28; p. 66.

16. Quoted in Devlin, *op. cit.*, p. 191.

17. Quoted in Brittain, *op. cit.*, pp. 55-56.

18. Devlin, *op. cit.*, p. 192.

19. Edith Sitwell, ed. *The Pleasures of Poetry* (New York, 1930), p. 78.

Chapter Three

1. Quoted in *Ainsworth and Noyes, op. cit.*, p. 10.

2. Cyril Falls, *The Critic's Armoury* (London, 1924), p. 110.

3. Devlin, *op. cit.*, p. 27.

4. The following analysis of Smart's early poetry according to form depends on Ainsworth and Noyes, *op. cit.*, pp. 50-56.

5. Quoted in Norman Callan, *The Collected Poems of Christopher Smart*, vol. I (London, 1949), p. xlviii (from the introduction to Mrs. Le Noir's *Poems*, 1825).

6. Hunter, *op. cit.*, p. xxxv.

7. Geoffrey Grigson, *Christopher Smart* (London, 1961), p. 9.

8. Brittain, *op. cit.*, p. 64.

9. Quoted in Ainsworth and Noyes, *op cit.*, p. 81.

10. Grigson, *op. cit.*, pp. 10-11.

11. *Ibid.*, pp. 12-13.

12. Devlin, *op. cit.*, p. 76. Devlin interprets the *Hymn to the Supreme Being*, pp. 77-78, and some of his findings are noted here.

Chapter Four

1. W. H. Bond, ed. *Jubilate Agno* (London, 1954). For the preceding remarks on the discovery and structure of the poem, Bond's Introduction, pp. 16-23, has furnished the material. The following analysis of the fragments is largely based on Bond's arrangement and interpretation.

2. Devlin, *op. cit.*, p. 114.

3. Quoted in Brittain, *op. cit.*, p. 42.

4. Quoted in Devlin, *op. cit.*, p. 19.

5. Note to the author from George Barker, March, 1967.

Chapter Five

1. Devlin, *op. cit.*, p. 138.

2. Quoted in Ainsworth and Noyes, *op. cit.*, p. 107.

3. *Ibid.*

4. Hunter, *op. cit.*, p. xliii.

5. Robert Browning, "With Christopher Smart," *Parleyings with Certain People of Importance in Their Day, The Complete Works of Robert Browning*, ed. Charlotte Porter and Helen A. Clarke, XII (New York, 1898).

6. Brittain, *op. cit.*, p. 294. Brittain has cited the following possible sources of the *Song*, pp. 293-94.

7. Sophia Blaydes, *Christopher Smart as a Poet of His Time* (The Hague, 1966), pp. 293-94.

8. Christopher Smart, *A Song to David*, ed. J. B. Broadbent (Cambridge, 1960), "Commentary," p. 36.

9. *Ibid.*, Introduction, p. xvi.

10. Blaydes, *op. cit.*, p. 128.

11. Brittain, *op.cit.*, p. 294.

12. *Ibid.*

13. Frederico Olivero, "Il 'Canto a Davide' di Christopher Smart," quoted and reviewed by Brittain, *op. cit.*, pp. 295-97.

14. Raymond D. Havens, "The Structure of Smart's *Song to David*" (*Review of English Studies*, April, 1938), reviewed by Brittain, *op. cit.*, p. 297.

15. Blaydes, *op. cit.*, pp. 123-24.

16. Brittain, *op. cit.*, pp. 298-99.

17. *Ibid.*, p. 299.

18. Patrick Delany, *An Historical Account of the Life and Reign of David, King of Israel* (London, 1740-42), reviewed and quoted by Brittain, *op. cit.*, pp. 299-300.

19. Devlin, *op. cit.*, p. 140.

20. Brittain, *op. cit.*, pp. 300-301.

21. *Ibid.*, p. 310.

22. *Ibid.*, p. 302.

23. *Ibid.*, p. 305.

24. Devlin, *op. cit.*, p. 141.

25. *Ibid.*, pp. 148-49.

26. Brittain, *op. cit.*, p. 303.

27. *Ibid.*

28. *Ibid.*

29. Blaydes, *op. cit.*, p. 150.

30. *Ibid.*

31. Brittain, *op. cit.*, p. 305.
32. *Ibid.*
33. Brittain, *op. cit.*, p. 306.
34. Blaydes, *op. cit.*, p. 154.
35. Brittain, *op. cit.*, p. 309.
36. Blaydes, *op. cit.*, p. 158.
37. Brittain, *op. cit.*, p. 309.
38. Ainsworth and Noyes, *op. cit.*, p. 123.
39. Blaydes, *op. cit.*, pp. 163-64.
40. *Ibid.*, p. 166.
41. Devlin, *op. cit.*, p. 150.
42. Blaydes, *op. cit.*, p. 166.
43. Brittain, *op. cit.*, p. 309.
44. Devlin, *op. cit.*, p. 151.

Chapter Six

1. Devlin, *op. cit.*, p. 157.
2. *Critical Review,* XVIII (July, 1764), p. 79, quoted in Ainsworth and Noyes, *op. cit.*, p. 133.
3. Devlin, *op. cit.*, p. 158.
4. *Ibid.*, p. 159.
5. *Ibid.*, p. 160.
6. Christopher Smart, *The Works of Horace Translated into Verse* (London, 1767), remarks from Preface quoted in Brittain, *op. cit.*, p. 68.
7. *Ibid.*, from translation of Horace, quoted in Brittain, *op. cit.*, p. 69.
8. Brittain, *op. cit.*, p. 69.
9. *Ibid.*, p. 312.
10. *Ibid.*, p. 315.
11. *Ibid.*, p. 315.
12. *Ibid.*, pp. 316-17.

Chapter Seven

1. Bond, *op. cit.*, p. 15.
2. Quoted in Ainsworth and Noyes, *op. cit.*, p. 48.
3. *Ibid.*, p. 66.
4. *Ibid.*, p. 82.
5. Bond, *op. cit.*, p. 15.
6. Quoted in Ainsworth and Noyes, p. 129.
7. *Ibid.*

8. *Ibid.*

9. Mme Frances d' Arblay, *op. cit.,* p. 28.

10. Peter Davis, unpublished thesis "The Literary Reputation of Christopher Smart" (Boulder: The University of Colorado, 1962), p. 9. This chapter is indebted to Mr. Davis's thesis for organization and examples.

11. *Ibid.,* p. 10.

12. Quoted in Callan I, *op. cit.* p. xlviii.

13. George Gilfallen, "Introductory Essay to 'A Song to David,' " *Specimans with Memoirs of the Less-Known British Poets,* vol. III (Edinburgh, 1860), pp. 151-53.

14. Quoted in Callan, vol. I, *op. cit.,* p. xlix.

15. Quoted in Davis, *op. cit.,* p. 13.

16. Quoted in Ainsworth and Noyes, *op. cit.,* p. 107.

17. William Force Stead, ed., *Rejoice in the Lamb* (New York, 1939), pp. 48-49.

18. Davis, *op. cit.,* p. 28.

19. George Saintsbury, *A History of English Prosody from the Twelfth Century to the Present Day,* II (New York, 1961), p. 513.

20. Eric Partridge, *Eighteenth Century English Romantic Poetry* (Paris, 1924), pp. 98-101.

21. Sitwell, *op. cit.,* pp. 77-78.

22. Edmund Blunden, ed. *A Song to David . . .* (London, 1924), p. 21.

23. Lawrence Binyon, *The Case of Christopher Smart* (London, 1934), pp. 6-18.

24. Ainsworth and Noyes, *op. cit.,* p. 111.

25. Quoted in Callan, vol. I, *op. cit.,* pp. xxx-xxxi.

26. Bond, *op. cit.,* p. 15.

27. Marianne Moore in a comment sent to the author February 2, 1967.

28. Richard Eberhart in a statement given to the author June 27, 1969.

Selected Bibliography

PRIMARY SOURCES

1. Bibliography:

"A Bibliography of the Writings of Christopher Smart," by G. J. Gray, *Transactions of the Bibliographical Society*, VI. London: East and Blaydes, 1903.

2. Collected Works:

Poems of the Late Christopher Smart. Ed. Christopher Hunter, 2 vols. Reading: Smart and Cowslade, 1791. Omits *A Song to David* and various other poems, but includes a biographical sketch by Hunter, the poet's nephew.

The Collected Poems of Christopher Smart. Ed. Norman Callan, 2 vols. London: Routledge and Kegan Paul, 1949. Omits some of the translations and oratorios, and the Latin poems.

Poems by Christopher Smart. Ed. Robert Brittain, Princeton: Princeton University Press, 1950. A selection only, but with items from the *Horace, Hannah,* and *Abimelech.* An excellent critical edition, with notes and introduction.

3. Separate Works:

The Horation Canons of Friendship. "Being the Third Satire of the first book of Horace Imitated." London: J. Newbery, 1750.

On the Eternity of the Supreme Being. Cambridge: J. Bentham, 1750. The Seatonian prize poem, 1750.

On the Immensity of the Supreme Being. Cambridge: J. Bentham, 1751. The Seatonian prize poem, 1751.

An Index to Mankind: or Maxims Selected from the Wits of All Nations. London: T. Carnan, 1751.

Poems on Several Occasions. London: J. Newbery, 1752.

On the Omniscience of the Supreme Being. Cambridge: J. Bentham, 1752. The Seatonian prize poem, 1752.

The Hilliad: An Epic Poem. London: J. Newbery, 1753. Occasioned by a literary quarrel.

On the Power of the Supreme Being. Cambridge: J. Bentham, 1754. The Seatonian prize poem, 1753.

On the Goodness of the Supreme Being. Cambridge: J. Bentham, 1756. The Seatonian prize poem, 1755.

Hymn to the Supreme Being, on Recovery from a dangerous Fit of Illness. London: J. Newbery, 1756.

The Works of Horace, Translated Literally into English Prose. 2 vols. London: J. Newbery, 1756.

The Non Pareil: or, the Quintessence of Wit and Humor, London: T. Carnan, 1757. An anthology of Smart's contributions to *The Midwife,* or *The Old Woman's Magazine,* 1750-53.

A Song to David. London: Mr. Fletcher, 1763.

Poems, viz. Reason and Imagination. A Fable. London: Fletcher, 1763.

Modesty. London: Fletcher, 1763. With several other pieces.

A Translation of the Psalms of David. London: Dryden Leach, 1765. Includes *A Song to David.*

Hannah, An Oratorio. London: J. and B. Tomson, 1764.

The Works of Horace, translated into Verse. 4 vols. London: W. Flexney, 1767.

The Parables of Our Lord and Saviour Jesus Christ, Done into familiar verse . . . for the use and improvement of younger minds. London: W. Owen, 1768.

Hymns for the Amusement of Children. Third Edition. London: T. Carnan, 1775. No earlier edition known.

Rejoice in the Lamb. Ed. W. F. Stead. London: Oxford, 1939. The first publication of *Jubilate Agno.*

Jubilate Agno. Ed. W. H. Bond. London: Rupert Hart-Davis, 1954. The standard text, rearranged according to the sequence of the original manuscript.

SECONDARY SOURCES

AINSWORTH, EDWARD GAY and CHARLES E. NOYES. *Christopher Smart: A Critical and Biographical Study.* Columbia: The University of Missouri, 1943. Useful, thorough work combining biography, criticism; also much on Smart's literary reputation—especially the contemporary reception of his work.

BLAYDES, SOPHIA B. *Christopher Smart As a Poet of His Time.* The Hague, The Netherlands: Mouton and Co., 1966. Very thorough, well-done study of Smart's work. Valuable in its comment on eighteenth-century poetics in general and Smart's prosody in particular.

BINYON, LAWRENCE. *The Case of Christopher Smart.* London: Oxford University Press, 1934. Thorough examination of the *Song.*

BLUNDEN, EDMUND, Ed. *A Song to David with other poems.* London: Richard Corden-Sanderson, 1924. An "Address" comments on Smart and his poetry, especially the *Song.*
  Introduction. *Hymns for the Amusement of Children,* Oxford; Oxford University Press, 1947. Valuable commentary on Smart's *Hymns.* Comparison of Smart and Blake.

BOSWELL, JAMES. *Boswell's Life of Johnson.* Ed. L. F. Powell. Oxford: Oxford University Press, 1934. Contains some comment on Smart by Johnson.

BOTTING, ROLAND B. "Christopher Smart in London," *Research Studies of the State College of Washington,* VII (1939), 3-54. Discussion of the "Paper War" and the poet's reaction to his critics; also an account of Smart's many activities.
  "Johnson, Smart, and the 'Universal Visitor,'" *Modern Philology,* XXXVI (1939), 293-300. The story of Johnson's contributions to the periodical in Smart's behalf.

BREDVOLD, LOUIS I. "The Literature of the Restoration and the Eighteenth Century, 1660-1798." *A History of English Literature.* Ed. Hardin Craig. New York: Oxford University Press, 1950. Good, general look at the period.

BRITTAIN, ROBERT E. "Smart in the Magazines," *Library,* 4th Series, XXI (1941), 320-36. Account of Smart's work in contemporary periodicals with some other criteria used to identify his writings. A chart included shows Smart's magazine contributions.

BROADBENT, J. B., ed. *A Song to David,* Cambridge, England: Rampant Lions Press, 1960. Includes an introduction with some biography and criticism; a commentary divides the poem into outline form.

BROWNING, ROBERT. "With Christopher Smart." *Parleyings with Certain People of Importance in Their Day* in *The Complete Works of Robert Browning.* Ed. Charlotte Porter and Helen A. Clarke. Vol. XII. New York: Houghton Mifflin, 1898. Browning's celebration of *A Song to David* in this poem, written in 1887, helped inspire the rediscovery of Smart in the nineteenth century.
  Letters of Robert Browning Collected by Thomas J. Wise. Ed. Thomas L. Hood. New Haven: Yale University Press, Murray and Ryerson, 1933. Valuable in showing some of the late nineteenth-century reaction to the *Song.*

CHALMERS, ALEXANDER. "The Life of Christopher Smart." *The Works of the English Poets.* XVI. London: J. Johnson, 1810.

Contains selections from Smart's poetry and a biographical and critical introduction.

CLIFFORD, JAMES L. "The Eighteenth Century." *Contemporary Literary Scholarship, A Critical Survey.* Ed. Lewis Leary. New York: Appleton, 1958. Comments on the growth of Smart's reputation because of editions of *Jubilate Agno.*

D'ARBLAY, Mme FRANCES. *The Early Diary of Frances Burney.* Ed. Annie Raine Ellis. London: G. Bell and Sons, 1889. 2 vols. Diary of a young girl in eighteenth-century London; many references to well-known people of the day—among them, Christopher Smart.

DAVIS, PETER EVERETT. Unpublished thesis, "The Literary Reputation of Christopher Smart." Boulder: The University of Colorado, 1962. Excellent survey of the progress of the literary reputation of Smart, with special attention to twentieth-century criticism and biography.

DEVLIN, CHRISTOPHER. *Poor Kit Smart.* London: Rupert Hart-Davis, 1961. Interesting, valuable study of Smart as man and poet; contains some new critical and biographical findings.

DISRAELI, ISAAC. *The Calamities and Quarrels of Authors.* Ed. Benjamin Disraeli. New York: W. J. Widdleton, 1881. Contains an account of John Hill's feud with Smart, Fielding, and others.

DRINKWATER, JOHN. *A Book for Bookmen.* London: Dudan, Ltd., 1926. Contains a brief discussion of Smart's Seatonian poems.

FAIRCHILD, HOXIE NEALE. *Religious Trends in English Poetry.* II. New York: Columbia University Press, 1942. A discussion of Smart's religious verse, especially the *Song;* includes comment on Smart's treatment of nature and its Christian implications.

FALLS, CYRIL. *The Critic's Armoury.* London: Cobden-Sanderson, 1934. *A Song,* Smart's "one bright flower," shows no connection with any literary period, but comes straight from the man's inner consciousness.

GILFALLAN, GEORGE. "Introductory Essay to 'A Song to David.' " *Specimens with Memoirs of the Less-Known British Poets.* III. Edinburgh: J. Nichol, 1860. Illustrates the early nineteenth-century view of Smart as a drunken lunatic who scratched the *Song* on the walls of his cell with a key.

GOSSE, EDMUND. *Gossip in a Library.* London: W. Heineman, 1892. Some brief biographical comment, especially in relation to Smart's quarrel with Gray; includes some criticism of the *Song;* mentions some of the poet's other work.

GRAY, G. J. "A Bibliography of the Writings of Christopher Smart, with Biographical References." *Transactions of the Bibliographical Society.* VI, ii. London: Blades, East and Blades, 1903.

Callan calls this work, "the definitive account of Smart's work, or at any rate of his poetry, the only important addition being the *Jubilate Agno.*"

GRIGSON, GEOFFREY. *Christopher Smart.* London: Longmans, Green and Co., 1961. Short biographical and critical study of Smart; some brilliant commentary on *The Hop-Garden,* the *Song,* and other of Smart's poems.

HAVENS, RAYMOND D. "The Structure of Smart's 'Song to David,' " *Review of English Studies,* XIV (1938), 327-52. Valuable analysis of the parallelism, formal design, and pattern of the *Song*—of the grouping of the stanzas in threes and sevens or their multiples. While the *Song* may have Romantic overtones, it also has "the ordered beauty of classic and neo-classic art."

JONES, CLAUDE. "Christopher Smart, Richard Rolt, and the 'Universal Visitor,' " *Library,* XVIII (1937), pp. 212-13. Smart and Rolt as editors of the *Universal Visitor.*

McKENZIE, K. A. *Christopher Smart, sa vie et ses oeuvres.* Paris: N. K., 1924. Discussion of Smart's life with detailed analysis of his works—especially the *Song.*

McKILLOP, ALAN DUGALD. *English Literature from Dryden to Burns.* New York: Appleton-Century-Crofts, 1948. Illustrates trend of interest in Smart other than for the *Song* alone.

MERCHANT, W. MOELWYN. "Patterns of Reference in Smart's *Jubilate Agno,*" *Harvard Library Bulletin,* XIV (1960), 20-28. Discussion of the associative nature of the references in *Jubilate Agno;* concludes that this manuscript is much less disconnected than is generally supposed.

MOORE, MARIANNE. Commentary about Smart in a poem sent to the author, February 2, 1967.

MURRAY, JOHN MIDDLETON. *Discoveries.* London: W. Collins, 1924. Praises unity of the *Song.* Finds value in *Hymns and Spiritual Songs.*

NOYES, CHARLES. Unpublished thesis, "Materials for a Biography of Christopher Smart." Columbia: University of Missouri, 1940. While this work was superseded by *Christopher Smart: A Biographical and Critical Study* (1943), a study initiated by Professor Ainsworth and finished after his death by Mr. Noyes, the thesis contains some useful additional notes and references.

PARTRIDGE, ERIC. *Eighteenth Century English Romantic Poetry.* Paris: E. Champion, 1924. Includes an examination of Smart's verse, particularly the *Song;* special emphasis on prosody.

PIGGOTT, STUART. "New Light on Christopher Smart," *Times Literary Supplement* (June 13, 1929), p. 474. A copy of the contract between Smart, Rolt, and Gardner shows that the terms were much fairer than implied by Johnson.

PRICE, CECIL. "Six Letters by Christopher Smart," *Review of English Studies*, VIII (1957), 144-48. Addressed to Smart's friends and benefactors, these letters reveal something of Smart's financial struggle and add to the material about the poet as a man.

ROGERS, K. M. "The Pillars of the Lord: Some Sources of *A Song to David*," *Philological Quarterly*, XL (1961), 525-34. This study helps to explain some of the passages of the *Song*. Rogers suggests the *Talmud*, the *Cabala*, and Masonic lore as possible sources of the *Song*.

SAINTSBURY, GEORGE. *A History of English Prosody from the Twelfth Century to the Present Day*. II. New York: Russell and Russell, 1908. Comments on Smart's poetry, especially the prosody of the *Song*.

SAMPSON, GEORGE. *The Concise Cambridge History of English Literature*. Cambridge, England; Cambridge University, 1941, Contains some remarks about the *Song* and some of Smart's other verse; links Smart with Blake.

SECCOMBE, THOMAS. *The Age of Johnson*. London: G. Bell and Sons, 1914. Seccombe comments on Smart's *Song* and *Hymns;* sees Smart as a forerunner of Blake.

"Smart, Christopher." *Dictionary of National Biography*. Ed. Sidney Lee. LII. London: Oxford University Press, 1897. Important early milestone in biography and criticism of Smart and his works.

SHEPARD, ODELL and PAUL SPENCER WOOD, eds. *English Prose and Poetry*. Boston: Houghton Mifflin, 1934. Full commentary on the *Song*. Shows some of the reaction toward the poem in its nineteenth-century revival. Commentators of the poem missed the mark both in blame and in praise. Thomas Campbell in *Specimens of the British Poets* (1801) is too derogatory. Dante Gabriel Rosetti is too strong in his praise when he calls the *Song* "the only great accomplished poem of the last century." Many of Rosetti's judgments, however, are very acceptable. Excerpts of the *Song* do not do justice to the poem's logical structure. Smart as a whole was closer to Keats than to Milton because "he made words do a double and treble duty . . . . He saw nature not in Keats's way, as a spectacle, but with the ecstatic innocence and freshness of vision which we associate with Traherne, Vaughn, and Blake."

SHERBO, ARTHUR. *"Jubilate Agno:* The Mind of Christopher Smart," *Papers of the Michigan Academy of Science, Arts, and*

Letters, XLV (1960), 421-25. Seeks to prove that Smart was capable, when confined, of thinking in an orderly and logical way.

———. "Survival in Grub Street: Another Essay in Attrition," *Bulletin of the New York Public Libraries,* LXIV (1960), 147-58. Sherbo, in his examination of Smart's canon, suggests that Smart did not write more poetry on the level of the *Song* because he was forced to work so hard for survival.

———. *Christopher Smart: Scholar of the University.* East Lansing: Michigan State University, 1967. Excellent biography. Examines all of Smart's important work. New commentary. Describes anti-David quarrel in the eighteenth century of which Smart was doubtless aware.

SHERBURN, GEORGE. "The Restoration and Eighteenth Century (1660-1789)." *A Literary History of England.* Ed. Albert C. Baugh. New York: Appleton-Century-Crofts, 1948. Excellent survey of the period with biographical and critical comment concerning the writers. Observes the rambling quality of the *Song,* but believes it is unique in the century in "sustained lyrical intensity, in bold transitions from the homely to the sublime, in exotic imagery, and in its piercing, mystical quality."

SIDE, KARINA. "Christopher Smart's Heresy," *Modern Language Notes,* LXIX (1954), 316-19. Smart's religious view of trichotomy, the idea that man is the image of the Holy Trinity, was not in conflict with the tenets of the Anglican Church, of which Smart was a member.

SITWELL, EDITH, *ed. The Pleasure of Poetry.* New York: Norton, 1930. Includes a reprinting of the *Song,* which Sitwell calls "a really great and entirely underrated poem," with critical comment.

STEAD, WILLIAM FORCE. "Smart's Metrical Psalms," *Times Literary Supplement* (October 22, 1938), p. 677. Discusses the writing of the Psalms and the poet's difficulty in getting someone to write music for them.

WILLIAMSON, KARINA. "Christopher Smart's *Hymns and Spiritual Songs,*" *Philological Quarterly,* XXXVIII (1959), 413-24. Detailed study of Smart's hymns; includes a comparison of his work with that of contemporary hymn-writers.

WOOD, FREDERICK T. "Christopher Smart," *Englische Studien,* LXXI (1936-1937), 191-213. Biographical and critical article; examines not only the *Song* but some minor poems. While Wood likes some of the minor works, he concludes that the *Song* was what Smart would and should be remembered for. The poet's work is dull as a whole but has many inspired lines.

Index

Addison, Joseph, 17, 18, 19

Blake, William, 5, 6, 21, 111, 119, 123, 135
Bond, W. W. H., 70, 71, 114, 118, 126
Boswell, James, 18, 36, 48, 116
Browning, Robert, 36, 79, 115, 116, 117, 119, 127, 132
Burney, Charles, 42, 45, 51, 52, 75
Burney, Frances, 51, 115, 126, 132

Carnan, Anna-Maria (Mrs. Christopher Smart), 13, 32-34, 40, 49, 51, 64, 70
Carnan, Thomas (Smart's brother-in-law), 12, 42, 43, 51, 52, 109
Cowper, William, 5, 6, 18, 19-21, 70
Critical Review, The, 44, 47, 51, 77, 78, 105, 114, 115

Delany, Patrick, 26, 80, 86, 87, 127
Delaval family (patrons), 31, 42, 45, 49, 105, 108

Gentleman's Magazine, The, 12, 34, 35, 36, 56, 113
Gray, Thomas, 18, 19, 20, 27, 32, 40, 42, 43, 78

Hawkesworth, John, 45, 46
Hill, John, 32, 34, 44, 113
Hunter, Christopher (nephew of Smart), 22, 23, 26, 27, 39, 57, 78, 115, 125

Johnson, Samuel, 12, 18, 19, 20, 31, 34, 36, 37, 40, 42, 75, 132
Jubilate Agno, 7, 13, 24, 33, 34, 37, 41, 43, 48, 69-77, 80, 85, 86, 89, 91, 114, 118, 121, 122, 123, 134, 135, 136

Kenrick, William, 12, 31, 34, 42, 103, 104, 113

137

Mason, William, 40, 42, 43, 44, 48, 50, 78
Midwife, The, 12, 30, 31, 36, 39, 112, 113
Miltonics, 19, 56, 57, 59, 66
Monthly Review, The, 44, 47, 89, 113-15

Neo-Classicism, 19, 20, 21, 108, 112, 123
Newbery, John, 11, 12, 13, 29-37, 39, 40, 42, 43, 46, 47, 49

Pope, Alexander, 11, 19, 20, 25, 49, 56, 112

Rolt, Richard, 30, 36, 42, 134

Sheratt, John, 41, 42, 65, 77, 103
Smart, Christopher; background (eighteenth century), expansion of the
    empire, 15; science, 16; social and political attitudes, 16, 17; literary
    scene, 17-20; birth, 22, 23; family, 22, 23; early education and life
    at Ruby castle, 23, 24; residence and writings at Cambridge, 24-28,
    55, 56; move to London and early writings, 28-31, 55, 56; early
    publication of poetry, 31, 32; marriage, 32-34; last writings before
    confinement, 34-36; madness and confinement, 37-41; release, 41;
    publications after release from confinement, 42-45; arrest and
    rescue, 48; last days before imprisonment, 49-51; imprisonment and
    last period before death, 51, 52; death,52.
WRITINGS (excluding *A Song to David* and *Jubilate Agno*):
    Abimelech, 13, 49, 109; Ballads, 63-64; Epigrams, Epitaphs, and
    Fables, 59-63, 103; *Hannah: An Oratorio,* 13, 44, 109, 118; *Hilliad,
    The,* 12, 32, 112; *Hop-Garden, The,* 23, 57-59, 134; *Horation
    Canons of Friendship, The,* 11, 64; *Hymns and Spiritual Songs,* 41,
    82, 106, 111, 119, 136; *Hymns for the Amusement of Children,* 14,
    52, 109-11, 121; *Hymn to the Supreme Being on Recovery from a
    Dangerous Fit of Illness,* 12, 38, 39, 68-70, 82, 116, 123, 126; *Mrs.
    Midnight's Orations,* 13, 41, 44, 75; *Occasional Prologue and
    Epilogue to Othello, An,* 12, 31, 113; Odes, 11,13,24,28,31,32,44,
    54-56, 103; *Ode to the Earl of Northumberland,* 13, 44, 104; *Old
    Woman's Oratory, The,* 12, 31; *Parables of Our Lord, The,* 13, 50,
    108, 109; Pastorals, 56-57; *Poems, viz. Reason and Imagination,* 13,
    103; *Poems of the Late Christopher Smart, The* (ed. by Hunter), 22,
    115, 125; *Poems on Several Occasions* (1752), 12, 31, 32, 55, 112,
    113; *Poems on Several Occasions, viz. Munificence and Modesty*
    (1763), 13, 44, 104; *Poetical Translation of the Fables of Phaedrus,
    A,* 13, 45, 46, 105, 116, 118; *Rejoice in the Lamb* (ed. by W. F.
    Stead (1939)—the first publication of *Jubilate Agno*), 70, 80, 118,
    120; Satire and Verse Epistles, 64, 65, 103; Seatonian Prize Poems,
    11, 12, 26, 30, 31, 35, 39, 40, 65-68, 80, 82, 112, 113; *Translations*

of the Psalms, A, 13, 41-43, 45, 48, 78, 82, 105, 106, 115, 123, 128, 136; *Works of Horace Translated Literally into English Prose, The,* 12, 35, 36, 46, 80, 107, 108, 113, 116, 118; *Works of Horace Translated into Verse, The* 6, 13, 46, 49, 106-8, 118

Smart, Elizabeth Anne (Mrs. LeNoir), daughter of the poet, 33, 40, 47, 49, 116

Smart, Margaret (Mrs. Hunter), sister of the poet, 22, 42, 45, 46, 54

Smart, Marianne (Mrs. Cowslade), daughter of the poet, 33, 40, 42

Smart, Marianne (Mrs. Falkiner), sister of the poet, 24, 40

Song to David, A, 5, 6, 13, 41-45, 67, 69, 70, 73, 78-103, 106, 110, 111, 116-22, 124, 127, 129, 132-36

Stead, William Force, 70, 77, 80, 118, 122, 129

Student, The 11, 29, 30, 32, 36, 112

Universal Visitor, The 12, 25, 36, 37, 132, 134

Vane family (patrons), 24, 42, 55